A SERIES OF
NEW TESTAMENT
STUDY GUIDES

HEBREWS

HELPS FOR
READING AND UNDERSTANDING
THE MESSAGE

Bob Young

James Kay Publishing

Tulsa, Oklahoma

A Series of New Testament Study Guides
HEBREWS
Helps for Reading and Understanding the Message
ISBN 978-1-943245-13-0

www.bobyoungresources.com

www.jameskaypublishing.com
e-mail: sales@jameskaypublishing.com

Table of Contents

Preface to the Series

A number of factors have converged in my life as influences on my method of Bible study and Bible teaching. My undergraduate training in Bible and biblical languages served as the foundation for 25 years of full-time preaching ministry. During those years in ministry, I periodically took graduate coursework in an effort to stay fresh.

When I decided to pursue graduate education diligently, I already loved teaching from an exegetical viewpoint while paying special attention to the historical-cultural context and the grammatical-syntactical features of the biblical text. I had seen the healthy ways in which people respond to thoughtful efforts to explain and apply the message of the Bible. I had developed the habit of using that same kind of Bible study in my sermon preparation. For those reasons, I focused my graduate training in ministry dynamics and how to integrate academic studies with practical applications. Because I did graduate work while continuing full-time work in ministry, I was blessed to have a laboratory to apply and test what I was learning.

My years of teaching and administration in Christian higher education coupled with increased involvement in the world of missions have made me even more aware of the need to view the Bible, insofar as possible, outside one's own social, cultural, experiential, and religious backgrounds. My interpretative efforts today are influenced by my training and experience. I try to understand the biblical context, the historical-cultural context, and the literary context—vocabulary, genres, grammar, and syntax. I try to understand the original message of the author and the purpose of the text as first steps toward understanding the message of the text in today's world. I want to know what the text said and what it meant, so that I can know what it says and what it means today.

As I have prepared these study guides, I have constantly asked myself, "What would I want in a study guide to the biblical text?" I have been guided by this question, at times excluding technical details and academic questions, at other times including such items because of their value in understanding and communicating the text. Above all, I have tried to provide a practical study guide to put in clear relief what the text says as a first step toward valid interpretation of what the text means and how it should be applied today.

I wrote these guides with multiple readers in mind. There is little new in these volumes, but preachers and Bible class teachers will be helped with their study and review of the text. Christians who have an interest in the message of the Bible will be helped by the textual jewels and the summaries that are included. The initial motivation to prepare these volumes came from my desire to provide a resource that will be translated into Spanish, keeping in mind the needs of preachers, Bible teachers, and Christians who do not have access to the many resources and books that exist in English. A good way to describe these guides is that they are simple explanations designed to help with the task of understanding and applying the biblical text. A few technical details are included to help with understanding, to identify repeated words or themes, and to give insights into the message of the text. May God bless you in your desire and your efforts to understand and apply the message of the Bible!

Introduction to the Series

The Purpose of These Guides

To describe the publications included in this series as "Bible study guides" says something about their intended purpose. As guides, these little books do not attempt to answer every question that may arise in your study of the biblical text. They are not commentaries in the strictest sense of the word. The focus of these guides is distinct.

I have as a primary goal to encourage you to do your own study of the Bible. This series of study guides is designed to assist the Bible student with preliminary and basic exegetical work, and to suggest some study methods that will enrich your study and help you identify the message of the text—whether in a specific verse or paragraph, a larger context, or an entire book of the New Testament. A primary goal of these guides is to help you maintain a focus on the purpose and message of the original author. The message of the original writer should inform our understanding of the text and its application today. One should not think that the message and meaning of the text today would be significantly different than the message and meaning of the original document.

The title also says that these guides are "helps." I have tried to provide resources to guide and enrich your study, keeping the purpose of the original author in view. This desire has informed the content of these study guides. Many study guides exist and there is no need to write more books that basically have the same content. Generally, the information included in these guides is designed to help identify the purpose of the original author and the message of the Bible. In some passages, the information included in these guides will provide insights not readily available in other resources.

What Kinds of "Helps" Are Included in These Guides?

These study guides reflect how I organize and understand the text of the Bible, taking into account various exegetical factors such as syntax, grammar, and vocabulary. Along the way, I share some observations that may help clarify passages that are difficult to understand. I have not tried to comment on every passage where potential problems or differences in understanding exist. I have not noted every textual variant in the original text. At times these notes may seem to be unnecessary comments on passages where the meaning is clear; that probably means I am trying to share insights to deepen understanding and appreciation of the text. In other passages, some may ask why I have not included more comments or explanation. Such is the individualized nature of Bible study. The overall goal of my comments is to help maintain a focus on the original author's message and purpose for writing—the "what it said and what it meant" of the original author in the original context.

For each chapter, there is a "Content" section that usually includes a brief outline, followed by notes ("Study Helps") about the biblical text. The content sections of these guides, including how the text is divided and how paragraphs are described, are drawn from my own reading and analysis of the text and from a comparison of several translations. In only a very few cases does the outline provided in this guide vary from the majority opinion, and those cases are noted and the reasons given. In some chapters, there is an overview with introductory comments to help orient the student to the overall content and message of the chapter. In a few chapters, there are some additional observations. Often, a paraphrased summary is included as part of the textual notes or in a separate section after the study helps. As noted above, the comments are not intended to answer every question. In a few cases, I have addressed topics that are not treated in detail in other resources. Texts that are easily understood and matters that are customarily included in other resources are, for the most part, not treated in detail here.

A Useful Tool for Understanding the Message of the Bible

While the primary purpose of these guides is to assist in personal study of the biblical text, these guides will also serve the casual reader who wants to understand the basic message of the Bible. The guides are written in such a way that the reader can understand the general message of the text, along with some interesting and helpful details, simply by reading the guide. One might describe theses guides as a kind of "CliffsNotes" to the Bible, but they are intended as helps and should not be thought of as taking the place of Bible reading and Bible study.

How to Use This Bible Study Guide in Personal Bible Study

This guide is not intended to take the place of your own Bible reading and study but is intended to provide insights and suggestions as you read the Bible, and to be a resource that will help you check your understanding. **No specific translation of the biblical text is included in this guide.** Two goals influenced the decision not to include a translation of the biblical text. First, it is hoped that you will be encouraged to use your own study Bible. Second, these notes are designed to be helpful in biblical study regardless of the version the reader may prefer for personal Bible study.

My primary purpose is to make it easier for you the reader and student to analyze and understand the text. Ultimately, you are responsible for your own interpretation of the Bible and you cannot simply follow what a favorite preacher or commentator says. Often the study notes for a chapter or subsection of a chapter are followed by a brief summary of the content, focusing on the message.

Five Steps for Bible Study. The suggested process for effectively using these Bible study guides involves five steps. First, you should read an introduction to the book of the Bible you wish to study. The introductions provided in these guides will serve well. They are for the most part briefer than normal and do not cover every detail. In this series of guides, sometimes one introduction is provided to cover multiple books, as in the case of the Thessalonian correspondence and the Pastoral Letters.

The second step in your study is to read through the book of the Bible you wish to study to understand the overall content. It will be helpful if this can be done at a single sitting. The student facing time constraints may have time for only one reading, but multiple readings will reveal additional details of the book, providing you an opportunity to notice repeated words and phrases and to think about the message of the book, how the book develops its message, and how various parts of the book are connected. You will find help for your reading in the chapter outlines that are provided in these study guides.

Now you are ready to begin your study of individual chapters or sections. The process is simple: read a section of the text until you have a good understanding of it. This step is not an in-depth reading to resolve every question but is a general reading to understand the content of the passage.

The fourth step is for you to write your own outline of the chapter or section, with paragraphing that reflects major thought patterns, divisions, and topics. In these study guides, each chapter has a section with suggested paragraphing based on a comparison of various translations. While it is possible to skip this step in which you do your own analysis and paragraphing, and to move directly to the paragraphing provided in the study guide, this is not the recommended approach. You will benefit from taking the time and investing the energy to do this work in initial reading and understanding.

Finally, the study guides have a section of study helps that will help you read and understand the text and keep the intent of the original author in mind as you do more focused study. In many chapters, a final section that summarizes the message of the chapter is included.

Initial Reading and Paragraphing

In other articles and publications, I have explained the importance of preparatory reading and personal study of the biblical text. In the five-step process described above, initial reading and paragraphing occur in the second, third, and fourth steps. When the student carefully works through these steps, it becomes clear that this is a "Bible" study and is not simply a process of reading more background information and commentary from a human author who is trying to explain the Bible. Although many students jump immediately from reading an introduction to reading a commentary, it is important that the student learn to read and study the Bible for herself or himself. Once the biblical text is familiar, I suggest the student think about the themes that can be identified and how to mark the paragraph divisions, based on the content of the passage and the subjects treated. Once this work is complete, it is good to compare the resulting paragraphing with that of several versions, or with the outlines in the content sections of these guides.

A Note About Paragraphing

Paragraph divisions are the key to understanding and following the original author's message. Most modern translations are divided into paragraphs and provide a summary heading. Ideally, every paragraph has one central topic, truth, or thought. Often, there will be several ways to describe the subject of the paragraph. Only when we understand the original author's message by following his logic and presentation can we truly understand the Bible. Only the original author is inspired—readers must take care not to change or modify the message. A first step toward integrity with the text is to develop the ability to analyze it and establish paragraphs.

Note: This introductory information is not repeated for each chapter. Students will find it helpful to return to this introductory section again and again to guide their study, especially before beginning the study of a new chapter of the Bible.

A Word About Formatting

The format of the Study Helps in each chapter follows the outline that is provided for the chapter. The major points of the outline are used to begin new sections of the Study Helps. Biblical references that introduce sections or subsections of the Study Helps are placed in bold type to assist the student. In the case of paragraphs that cover multiple verses, the biblical references are placed in progressive order on the basis of the first verse in the citation.

Standard abbreviations of biblical books are used. Verse citations that do not include the name of a book (e.g. 2:14) refer to the book being studied. Other abbreviations that may not be familiar to some readers include the following: cf. = compare; e.g. = for example; v. = verse; vv. = verses.

The first time a translation is mentioned, the standard abbreviation is included for translations that are less well-known. Subsequent references use only the abbreviation.

Greek words are placed in italics. Often, the corresponding Greek word, a literal meaning, and other translation possibilities are placed in parentheses immediately after an English word. Greek words are written as transliterations in English letters, using the basic lexical form of the word. It is hoped that this will make it easier for the reader without a knowledge of Greek. Many readers will find these references interesting, especially in the repeated use of the same Greek word. Readers can quickly pass over this inserted parenthetical information if desired. In a few cases, parentheses are used to indicate Greek verbal forms or noun forms, where this information would be significant to the student with some understanding of grammar. Again, the reader can pass over this information rapidly if desired. The Greek text used is the 27th edition of *Novum Testamentus Graece* which is identical with the 4th revised edition of *The Greek New Testament*.

Quotation marks are often used to call attention to special words or topics, and also to indicate citations or translations of the biblical text, most of which are my own. This is done to help the reader identify references to the biblical text, since no specific translation of the biblical text is included in this Study Guide.

Parentheses are used liberally to enclose information and comments that would often be included in footnotes. It is hoped that readers will find this more convenient, both those who want to read the expanded explanation and those who wish to skip over the parenthetical material.

Comments concerning contemporary applications of the text are limited, but are included from time to time.

Summaries are provided for many chapters, with the goal of helping to make the message of the chapter easier to identify. Some of these summaries are paraphrases, some are written in first person, from the standpoint of the author; others are written in third person and are explanations of the content. Summaries written in either the first person or third person are not translations and they are not paraphrasing. They are attempts to communicate the basic points and the purpose of the original message.

READING AND UNDERSTANDING
THE MESSAGE

Introduction to Hebrews

Summary

Hebrews is one of the great literary masterpieces of the New Testament. Some of the problems we encounter in understanding the book come from our tendency to put New Testament teaching into Pauline "pigeonholes." Hebrews is not a doctrinal statement concerning God's method of justification; it is an admonition to faithfulness in the face of difficult, threatening circumstances. It was not written to Christians in general but was written to a specific group of Christians who were struggling with questions about integrating two religious systems—is it possible, how, why, is it necessary, why cannot we return to the previous system? A great challenge in the study of Hebrews is to understand the contemporary parallels and applications for Christians today.

Some of the questions we struggle with in studying Hebrews would never have arisen in the minds of the first-century recipients and readers. Hebrews must be understood as occasional literature—written at a specific time and place to a specific group of people for a specific purpose in light of specific circumstances. The categories that are often superimposed on the book do not match the original circumstances. In reading the book of Hebrews, the contemporary church struggles with the challenge of hearing and understanding the message of the author. Understanding the book of Hebrews demands of us new categories in our theology and a renewed effort to listen to an inspired author. Sometimes, it demands that we learn to live with an interpretive tension we do not like.

The modern church desperately needs to hear the message of the book of Hebrews. The church needs to understand the completeness of God's plan in sending Jesus, resolving both the sin problem and the weakness problem. The church needs to hear that following God is not only evidenced by initial faith response but also by continuing faithfulness. Hebrews focuses on strength for the journey and persevering to the end more than on the beginning. The admonitions to be diligent, to be faithful, to grow up, to draw near to God, and not to miss God's grace are as fresh as ever. The message that faith is confirmed by our actions is an essential, often missing ingredient in the church today.

Introduction to the Book

Hebrews is filled with references to Old Testament texts. In the book of Hebrews, these Old Testament texts must be understood in the context of first-century rabbinical Judaism. The hermeneutic used to understand the book must consider first-century Jewish interpretative methods and avoid the tendency to think only in the patterns of modern Western thought. One description of the book is that it is a New Testament explanation of the Old Testament priestly system and covenant. Hebrews has been called the "Fifth Gospel."

Because Hebrews lacks the typical salutation it is often considered a homily or sermon. The conclusion of the book resembles a letter. The author calls the book a "word of exhortation" (13:22, see Acts 13:15 for the same phrase used as a description of a sermon). Modern translations that describe it as a letter go beyond what the text says and enter the realm of interpretation. Several commentaries note that the book is filled with warnings or admonitions. Five primary admonitions are often identified, but there are clearly other texts in Hebrews that fit the category. The primary admonitions, and many of the imperatives in the book, deal with the dangers of rejecting Jesus and returning to Judaism.

Authorship, Recipients, Date and Purpose

Author. The authorship of Hebrews is uncertain. The book was considered an authoritative Christian writing in the second century and is quoted in early Gnostic literature. The Alexandrian church accepted Paul's authorship although some Alexandrian church leaders recognized problems related to Paul's authorship of the book. Hebrews is listed in Paul's writings in the P^{46} papyrus manuscript from the second century. In this papyrus, Hebrews comes after Romans. The book is omitted from the list of Paul's letters in the Muratorian Fragment (a list of the books of the New Testament from Rome), dated about AD 180.

While the book is anonymous, the following seem clear: that the author was most likely a second-generation Christian (2:3), that the Old Testament citations come from the Septuagint, that the author wrote with classical Greek grammar and syntax, and that the author was known to and respected by the recipients of the book. The book demonstrates a high respect for the authority of the Old Testament.

Given that there are doubts about Paul's authorship—especially in view of stylistic and vocabulary differences and phrasing methods—the question that arises is, "Who did write the book?" Possibilities that have been suggested include Luke, Clement of Rome, Barnabas, Apollos, Philip and Silas. Ultimately, we return to our first statement: the authorship of the book is uncertain.

Recipients. The title of the book says that it is addressed "to the Hebrews." There is no internal reference in the text of the book to help us identify the recipients, that is, there is no internal reference to "the Hebrews." Whether the book was intended for a general audience or a specific group of Jewish Christians is not known. The recipients were apparently Jewish believers (consider the large number of Old Testament quotations) who had experienced persecution (10:32; 12:4). They had perhaps been Christians for some time, since the writer says they were still immature even though they should have developed spiritually (5:11-14). It may be that they were trying to mix Judaism and Christianity, that they were hesitant to make a clean break with Judaism (6:1-2), or that they were contemplating rejecting Christianity and returning to Judaism (10:26-31). The text of 13:24 is not helpful in identifying the recipients since it can be understood as "from Italy" or "to Italy," probably referring to Rome.

Date. As may be expected, with uncertainty concerning authorship and the situation of the recipients, there are also questions concerning the date. Hebrews is quoted by Clement of Rome in AD 95. A major question is whether the date of the book is before AD 70 or after. The evidence is inconclusive. Some have pointed out that temple worship is described in the present tense, possibly supporting a pre-AD 70 date, but the text in Revelation 11 also speaks of the temple in the present tense although few would date the book of Revelation before AD 70. The persecutions mentioned may favor a later date (after AD 70). On the other hand, some would see the reference to the "approaching day" in 10:25 as anticipating the destruction of Jerusalem.

Purpose. The following purposes have been suggested: encouragement to Jewish Christians to (1) leave Judaism and fully identify with the Christian community, (2) accept and share the word of Christ, (3) mature in faith, and (4) commit to Christian living and example. The admonitions that appear throughout the book focus on the need to develop and live out faith in Christ.

Brief Overview of Hebrews

This brief overview demonstrates how the book of Hebrews calls attention to and continually focuses on Jesus. One theme that summarizes the book is "The Superiority of the Son...."

- In comparison to the prophets, 1
- In comparison to the previous revelation, 1-2
- In comparison to the angels, 1-2
- In comparison to Moses, 3-4
- In comparison to Joshua, 4
- In comparison to the Aaronic priesthood, 5
- In comparison to the Old Testament high priesthood, 5-7
- Comparing the new covenant with the Old Testament law, 8-10
- Comparing access to the promise, 10-11
- Comparing access to the presence of God, 10-11
- Comparing the kingdoms, 12

The Development of the Message of Hebrews

In a series of graphics that appear throughout the book, this Bible study guide explains how the message of the book of Hebrews is advanced by the author. An overview of the outline is provided here to help the reader see that progression.

Chapter 1   **Jesus Christ, Son of God**
Jesus is greater than the prophets
Jesus is greater than the angels

         2:1-4   First Exhortation: Listen
Pay Attention to the Message

Chapter 2   **Jesus Christ, Son of Man**
Jesus became like human beings
Jesus is thus a faithful and merciful high priest

Chapter 3   **Jesus Compared to Moses**
Moses was a servant in the house of God
Under Moses, the people rebelled in disbelief
Under Moses, the people failed to enter the rest

       3:12-14   Second Exhortation: Be Faithful
Do Not Develop a Heart of Unbelief

Chapter 4   **The Rest Remains to be Entered**
Jesus compared to Joshua
Make every effort to enter that rest

4:14-16   **Jesus the Great High Priest**
4:14-7:28   A Better Ministry

Chapter 5   Jesus the Great High Priest (continued)
Chosen by God as a "Melchizedek High Priest"

       5:11-6:20   Third Exhortation: Maturity, Grow Up
Excursus: God's promise and oath

Chapter 7   A "Melchizedek High Priest"
8:1-6   "This is the point...."
8:6   Better ministry, better covenant, better promises

8:7-10:18   A Better Covenant

10:19-12:29   Better Promises

       10:22-25   Fourth Exhortation: Draw Near
12:14-16   Fifth Exhortation: Be Careful

Chapter 13   **Final Imperatives**

A Few Other Matters

In this volume, a summary of the message of the book appears in a separate section after Chapter 13. After the summary of the message, several sample studies and sermons are included to give examples of how to focus the message and how to move from the biblical text to the Bible class or sermon.

No footnotes are included in this volume because the content is considered general knowledge. No bibliography is supplied since I have worked primarily from the biblical text and my own notes.

This was the first volume I completed in the Bible Study Guides series. As I began the project, I searched for ideas about how to best accomplish what I had in mind for the series. That search led me to Bible studies prepared by Bob Utley. His format was helpful in the development of this volume. The influence of his wording, explanations, and approach is at times apparent.

Hebrews 1

[Note: it is suggested that the student read the introductory materials in this guide before beginning individual preparatory reading and analysis.]

CONTENT

The paragraphing included in the Content section of each chapter provides suggestions or guides for the reader. The reader is encouraged to identify the paragraphs and the subsections within each paragraph as part of his or her personal study. The division of the text into paragraphs is fairly standard in most translations.

Outline of Chapter

1:1-4, prologue, God has now spoken through a son, referring to Jesus the Son

1:5-14, the superiority of the Son to angels

Overview of Chapter

1:1-4. These verses contain a poetic description of Jesus in his divine, cosmic, and redemptive dimensions, although he is not mentioned by name. This text is one of several Christological passages in the New Testament (other well-known Christological texts are in John 1:1-18; Phil. 2:6-11; Col. 1:15-17). God has now spoken through a Son so that the partial revelation that came through the prophets has been replaced by the complete revelation that came through the Son (1:2; 3:6; 5:8; 7:28). The claim that Jesus is a son is supported by seven descriptions of Jesus.

1:5-14. The second major paragraph continues the theme. Not only is the revelation of Jesus superior to that of the prophets (1:1-4), he is superior to the angels. This truth is confirmed by a series of seven Old Testament citations from the Septuagint (mostly from the Psalms): Ps. 2:7; 2 Sam. 7:14; Ps. 97:7; 104:4; 45:6-7; 102:25-27; 110:1.

STUDY HELPS

1:1-4. It will be helpful to the student to notice at the beginning the seven descriptive phrases in this section. The son is described as....

1. heir (v. 2)
2. agent in creation (v. 2)
3. radiance of the Father's glory (v. 3)
4. exact image of the Father's essence (v. 3)
5. sustainer of the creation (v. 3)
6. means of forgiveness (v. 3)
7. exalted (v. 3)

The construction of the first sentence (vv. 1-2) is as follows: "In many portions and in various ways before, God having spoken to the fathers by the prophets, in these last days he spoke to us by a son, whom he established heir of all things, through whom also he made the world."

The word order and parallel construction suggest that this text is about the method of revelation in the past in comparison to the revelation given by a son. The phrase "in the prophets" is parallel to the phrase "in a son," calling attention to the comparison of the two methods of revelation. The first revelation came through servants, the second came through a son. The Jews believed that the prophets wrote Scripture. That truth provides a beginning point to understanding the significance of this introductory statement. The initial phrase calls attention to the partial nature of the Old Testament revelation, both in content and in form. The Old Testament prophets had a partial message that came in bits and pieces, from time to time, in various places, in various ways, by various people, in various forms.

While there are disagreements about the meaning of the phrase "in these last days," it is most likely that the primary point being made by the author is that God's revelation through Jesus Christ has come at the end of the days of Judaism. The phrase "last days" is used repeatedly in the Old Testament to refer to the end of the Jewish dispensation. In the New Testament, the phrase is also used to refer to a time period in the Christian dispensation. The Old Testament Jews were anticipating the coming of an age of righteousness that would begin with the coming of the Messiah. Whether one understands the last days as preceding AD 70 and the end of the Jewish dispensation, or as extending beyond AD 70 with the Son speaking through the inspired written word, the point of the author is unchanged. The time has come when God's revelation through the prophets has been replaced by the revelation given through the Son.

A word should be said about the use of the phrase "the Son." In the original text, the use is anarthrous (grammatically speaking, without an article), reminding us that the point is the manner of revelation. God's revelation is not coming through servants like the angels, Moses or the prophets, but through a son. I have used both "a son" and "the Son" in these comments. Sometimes the anarthrous noun in Greek serves to communicate an abstract concept. The reference is obviously to Jesus, although he is not mentioned by name until 2:9. The point of the text is that the revelation of God in the last days is given through one who exists in the closest relationship possible with the Father. Because Jesus is a son, the seven descriptions that follow are true. These show that this son (Jesus) is indeed the Son of God.

In the first two of the seven descriptions, two things are affirmed: "God appointed him heir of all things, and through him God made the world." In the normal course of events, sons are heirs. This phrase affirms that Jesus is a son. The idea that God appointed Jesus heir must not be understood in a way that demeans or depreciates the eternal deity of Jesus. Jesus as heir predates his Incarnation as is clear in the next phrase. He is heir and therefore he is uniquely Son of God. The text also affirms that the world was made through him (compare John 1:1-3). How the members of the Godhead worked together in the creation is not revealed, but this verse clearly affirms the presence and involvement of both Father and Son. The Greek word *aionos* (world) can refer to both physical matter and time. Jesus created both. The writer of Hebrews uses *aionos* and *kosmos* synonymously to describe the world (1:2; 6:5; 11:3; 4:3; 9:26; 10:5; 11:7, 38).

1:3. Continuing the descriptions, v. 3 completes the list with five more truths about Jesus: Jesus is the radiance of God's glory, the exact representation of God's nature, upholding all things by the word of his power. He made purification; he was exalted.

"The radiance of his glory." The word translated as "radiance" is also translated as brightness or reflection. This occurrence is the only use of this Greek word in the New Testament. The Hebrew *kabod* (glory) carries with it the sense of brightness. The Hebrew word *kabod* can refer to a pair of scales, reflecting the root meaning of "heaviness." The word thus comes to mean "having value or worth." Sometimes the idea of brightness (Hebrew, *shekinah*) is combined with glory to express God's majesty. To say that Jesus reflects God's glory may refer to righteousness, holiness, or the image of God shared also with human creation.

"The representation of his essence." Jesus is the exact representation (image or likeness) of God's nature (essence). This phrase is found only here in the New Testament. Here the Greek word is *charakter*; in 2 Cor. 4:4 and Col. 1:15 the same basic idea is communicated with the Greek word *eikon* (icon). The latter word is more common in the New Testament, but the idea in Heb. 1:3 is stronger. The word "essence" combines the concepts of "standing" and "under." The nature or essence is that which "stands under," meaning that which supports, defines, or gives value (cf. 3:14 and 11:1 where the same Greek word is used).

"Sustaining all things...." Jesus upholds (maintains, sustains) all things (cf. Col. 1:17) by the word of his power. God created by the spoken word. The word has the force and the capacity necessary to accomplish God's will. Jesus is called the "Word" in John 1:1 but the "word" here does not refer to Jesus. A study of the biblical concept of the "word" and its various uses is beyond the scope of this study.

"Having made purification." Jesus made purification (middle voice, aorist indicative) referring the action of purification back to the subject (Jesus) and describing a completed act. This Greek word provides the root for the English word "catharsis" and refers to the expiation and forgiveness of sins made possible through Jesus. The purification of sins communicates that Jesus dealt with the presence of sin in the world, which presence is evident in individual acts of sin. The plural suggests a reference to the sins of all humanity.

"He sat down...." Jesus was exalted when he finished his work on earth. Such exaltation suggests a kingly, royal role but is also linked to his priestly function. Jesus is prophet, priest, and king. This idea runs through these introductory verses and is a major point that will be developed by the author. These three functions of Jesus can be seen in numerous Old Testament passages.

1:4. This verse provides a bridge from the introductory paragraph to the supporting evidence that the author of Hebrews will cite. The things already mentioned make clear that Jesus is better than the angels, and therefore he has inherited a more excellent name than they. Jesus' name is greater than the angels, given that he is also "son" and "Lord."

Here is introduced the theme of greater (better, superior, more excellent) that recurs throughout the book (1:4; 6:9; 7:7, 19, 22; 8:6; 9:23; 10:34; 11:16, 35, 40; 12:24).

1:5-14. As there were seven descriptive phrases, the author now proves his point concerning the superiority of the Son (v. 4) with the use of seven Old Testament citations.

"To which of the angels did he ever say, you are my son, today have I begotten you." The first passage quoted to prove the superiority of the Messiah over the angels is Ps. 2:7. This was a royal psalm with primary application to the kings of the Old Testament, but it was also understood as a Messianic psalm. The phrasing is used in the New Testament numerous times to refer to Christ. The additional phrase "today I have begotten you" refers to Jesus' deity (John 1:1-18). Jesus is superior to the angels as begotten son (cf. John 3:16). The argument the author of Hebrews makes in citing this text is an "argument from silence." It is based on what the Father never said. The angels are not sons because of what God never said. Because it was never said, the idea is to be rejected.

"I will be a Father to him, and he will be to me a son." This phrase comes from 2 Sam. 7:14 and originally referred to Solomon. (A parallel use of an Old Testament prophecy with dual applications is seen in Isa. 7:14. The prophecy in Isaiah was fulfilled in its historical context, but Matthew applies it to Jesus.) The author uses 2 Sam. 7:14 to show that Jesus is superior to the angels because God claims him as son and is thus Father to him.

"And again, when he brings (sends) the firstborn into the world, he says, let all the angels of God worship him." This quotation is either from Deut. 32:43 or Ps. 97:7, the latter is more probable. This text refers to the Incarnation, not to a future coming of Jesus the Son. Notice the literary introduction of a new phrase or quote (compare v. 5d; 2:13; 4:5; and 10:30). Firstborn is a reference to preeminence (cf. Rom. 8:29; Col. 1:15, 18; Rev. 1:5) and does not imply that the son had a beginning, that is, that he was created. The phrase "into the world" not only reflects the Incarnation but also speaks to the preexistence of Jesus who has always been deity. For "world," note the use of *oikoumene* instead of the more common *kosmos* (cf. 2:5). The point of the author is that Jesus is shown to be superior because angels worship him.

The next quotation combines two Old Testament texts from Ps. 104:4 and Ps. 45:6, and develops the contrast between the angels who are not unchanging and Jesus who is permanent and unchanging. This theme appears in other places in the book of Hebrews and will become an important part of understanding Jesus' high priesthood. "He said to the angels, he who makes the angels his spirit and his ministers of fire. But to the son, your throne, O God, is forever. Your kingdom is a rod of uprightness." The second part of the quotation from Psalm 45 is clearly Messianic in its Old Testament context. Despite some ambiguity and a textual variant in the Greek manuscript, here is a clear affirmation of the deity of Christ. The "forever" throne is eternal. Jesus is superior to the angels because he is permanent and unchanging.

"You have loved righteousness and hated iniquity; therefore, God, thy God, hath anointed you with the oil of gladness above your companions." This quotation from Ps. 45:7 continues the quotation immediately above. The writer is describing the life and ministry of Jesus as the anointed (chosen, Messiah) of God. The phrase "above your companions" may simply finish the quotation, but in the context, one may also see Jesus' superiority over the Old Testament prophets and the angels, or one may see a foreshadowing of Jesus' superiority in the matters yet to be addressed in the book. Jesus is superior to the angels because of the work he did as God's "Anointed One."

"You, Lord, in the beginning did lay the foundation of the earth and the heavens are the works of your hands. They shall perish but you continue, they wax old like a garment and you will roll them up as a mantle. They will be changed as a garment but you are always the same and your years never end." This quotation begins with a citation from Ps. 102:25. In the Psalms text, Lord is YHWH, but in the context of Hebrews the quotation refers to Jesus, giving additional support to the previous reference to Jesus as God. Jesus is portrayed as participant in the creation, the Father's agent in creation (see 1:2). The point of the quotation is that Jesus is eternal in comparison to the created order—a creation that would include the angels as created beings. The writer affirms the permanence and stability of God's throne and God's Son. The latter part of the quotation is from Ps. 102:27, showing the immutability of Jesus (see 13:8). Again, the contrast is with the changeability of the created order. The permanence of Jesus' person is affirmed as evidence of his superiority to the angels.

The Development of the Message of Hebrews

Chapter 1   Jesus Christ, Son of God
Jesus is greater than the prophets
Jesus is greater than the angels

2:1-4   First Exhortation: Listen
Pay Attention to the Message

Chapter 2   Jesus Christ, Son of Man
Jesus became like human beings
Jesus is thus a faithful and merciful high priest

"To which of the angels did he ever say, sit at my right hand until I make your enemies your footstool. Are they not rather ministering spirits sent to serve those who shall inherit salvation?" This Old Testament quotation is from Ps. 110:1, a Messianic psalm that is frequently cited or alluded to in Hebrews (cf. 1:3, 13; 5:6, 10; 6:20; 7:3, 11, 17, 21; 8:1; 10:12-13; 12:2). This argument is also based on silence—that which God did not say. The point of the quote is that the angels exist to serve God and mankind. Humans are a higher order of creation than the angels (1 Cor. 6:3). In 2:14-16, the author will point out that

Jesus did not become like the angels in order to redeem them, but that he took on human form.

These seven quotations from the Old Testament provide the foundation for the claim of the writer of Hebrews: Jesus as Son of God is superior to the angels.

Hebrews 2

[Note: it is suggested that the student read the introductory materials in this guide before beginning individual preparatory reading and analysis.]

CONTENT

The paragraphing included below, and in the Content section of each chapter, serves only to give suggestions. The student is encouraged to read the text and identify the paragraphs and subsections of the paragraph as part of her or his own study. In this chapter, the division of the biblical text into paragraphs is fairly standard in modern translations.

<u>Outline of Chapter</u>

2:1-4, exhortation not to miss the great salvation
Note: this is the first of five major exhortations.
2:5-18, Jesus "made lower" and exalted to bring salvation to humanity

>**2:5-8**, a description of God's actions and intent for humanity in general (from Psalm 8)
>**2:9-10**, the same truths applied to Jesus
>**2:11-13**, the sanctifier and the sanctified are of the same nature and of the same family
>**2:14-16**, Jesus came in human likeness, not in the form of angels
>**2:17-18**, the summary: Jesus can thus be a faithful and merciful high priest, capable of atoning for sins and capable of understanding and helping in times of trouble.

<u>Overview of Chapter</u>

The first two chapters of Hebrews are a single literary unit. Chapter 1 makes clear the superiority of the revelation, nature, and work of Jesus as Son of God (1:1-4), and Jesus' superiority over the angels (1:5-14). Chapter 2 connects Jesus with humanity, identifying him as Son of Man, the one who tasted death for all human beings (2:9-10). He is thus a capable high priest (2:17-18), faithful and merciful, qualified to be the source of human salvation and able to identify with and understand the human dilemma.

The major emphasis of Chapter 2 is Jesus' connection with humanity. Because Jesus identifies with human beings, they can share his glory. Humanity can be restored to glory, honor and dominion through Jesus who is the ideal human (2:5-9).

Chapter 2 contains the first in a series of exhortations or warnings in the book of Hebrews (2:1-4; 3:12-14; 5:11-14; 10:22-25; 12:14-16). The first warning (2:1-4) is based on the teachings in the first chapter. The Jews understood that the Old Testament was given through angels. Therefore, based on the evidence that Jesus is superior to the angels, the words of Jesus are to be followed with even greater diligence.

STUDY HELPS
2:1-4. "Therefore" refers to what was said in the first chapter. These verses contain the first of five major exhortations in the book of Hebrews. This warning occurs in the middle of the first literary unit (Chapters 1-2).

First Exhortation
Therefore, it is necessary to pay even greater attention to the things we have heard so that we do not drift past them. For if the message spoken by angels was sure and every violation and disobedience received its just recompense, how shall we escape if we are neglectful of a salvation as great as this, which was first spoken by the Lord, and was confirmed to us by those who heard him.
--Hebrews 2:1-3

It is necessary to pay closer attention (*prosecho*, hold firmly) to the truths of the revelation or message that comes through Jesus. The verb means to give complete attention. The warning contains two nautical metaphors. The first occurs in the phrase "to give diligent attention." This phrase was used of bringing a ship to land. The second occurs in the phrase "so we do not drift away from it" or "so we do not slip by." The word was used figuratively of water currents or wind causing a ship to miss the port.

The content of the book of Hebrews suggests four possible problems: some were rejecting the gospel (2:3), some had believed but failed to mature (compare 2:1 and 5:11-14), some had believed but were incorporating Judaism into their faith system, and some were leaving Christianity and returning to the Jewish system.

Verse 2 begins with a first class conditional clause indicating that the statement is considered true—sometimes translated "since" or "because." The Jews accepted that the Old Testament word of God was spoken through angels and that it contained penalties for transgressions and disobedience. The "message spoken by angels" refers to the Mosaic Law. The Mosaic Law demanded obedience. That being true, the question of v. 3 naturally follows: If ignoring God's truth led to punishment in times past, how will it be possible to escape when one neglects (*ameleo,* not to pay attention, making light of, not regarding) the word of God spoken in these last days through the Son? Recognizing that there has not yet been any mention of covenants, but in anticipation of what is to come, the question could be worded like this: "If neglecting God's word under the first covenant had dire consequences, will not those consequences be even more severe under the new and better covenant inaugurated through the Son?" The consequences of willful neglect or rejection are also the subject of Hebrews 10:26-31.

In v. 3, the author includes himself among those who had received the message of the Lord from others, making him a second-generation Christian. This reference is generally thought to exclude the apostles, including Paul, from the list of potential authors. (But see other uses of "we" in the book where the writer may not be included with the recipients, especially 10:26-31.) This message was first announced by the Lord.

2:4. The message was validated and confirmed with signs and wonders, miracles, and gifts of the Holy Spirit, through which God himself gave testimony to the truth of message. These confirm for the believer the validity of the message.

2:5-8. God did not subject the world to angels. God's eternal plan is focused on the human creation made in his image and likeness. To support this truth, the writer cites Ps. 8:4-6, followed by several other Old Testament quotations in Chapter 2. The wording of 2:6 does not indicate that the author did not know the location of the citation, but is a way of referring to the inspired Scripture of the Old Testament.

In the book of Hebrews, the citation and descriptions in vv. 6-8 do not refer to Jesus but to the human creation. The text of Psalm 8 and its use in this passage deserve close attention. The Hebrew phrase "son of man" is an idiom to refer to humanity, an idiom that is picked up in the New Testament and used with reference to the Messiah. The word for angels in the Hebrew text of Psalm 8 is "Elohim," explaining why some translations read, "You have made him a little less than divine" or "less than God." The Septuagint (LXX) translates "angels" and this translation is followed by the author of Hebrews.

Some have translated "little" as a time reference— "you have for a little time made him lower…." Because the same construction is repeated with reference to Jesus (v. 9), seeing "little" as a time reference seems preferable. A textual variant does not include the reference to dominion over creation. Regardless of the textual or translation difficulties, the point is that human beings were crowned with the glory and honor of God and were given dominion over the creation (vv. 7-8). This statement refers back to the creation account in Genesis 1-2. The theological point is that Jesus and his followers are superior to the angels (compare 1:14).

Verse 8 focuses the difficulty the writer of Hebrews wishes to address. While God gave dominion to humankind and made all things subject to human beings, there is an exception. The context of the verses that follow makes clear that the writer is referring to death. Death is not subject to human control.

2:9-10. In this verse the author applies the quotation from Psalm 8 to Jesus as the ideal and perfect representative of humanity. Mankind was given authority, glory and honor, but with the entry of sin in the Garden, death also entered, destroying at least in part that authority, glory and honor. Jesus fulfills what God intended for humanity originally. Jesus in his Incarnation participates in the human experience, lowered for a little time, crowned with glory and honor through suffering death on behalf of all. Here is the first reference to Jesus by name in the book. In Hebrews, the name Jesus is most often used without additional description (2:9; 3:1; 6:20; 7:22; 10:19; 12:2, 24; 13:12), perhaps focusing on his capacity to save as high priest (the name Jesus means Savior). This possibility provides a contrast with the experience of God's people under the leadership of Moses and Joshua (Joshua is the Hebrew form of the name Jesus). Joshua did not give God's Old Testament people rest in the Promised Land, but Jesus brings God's people to a complete rest that fulfills the connection between God's seventh day rest and the true meaning of Sabbath.

This Jesus did through suffering death, a clear reference to Old Testament teaching concerning the Messiah (e.g., Psalm 22 and Isaiah 53). His suffering on behalf of all was by God's grace. Suffering was God's will for Jesus. Here is a clear statement of the vicarious, substitutionary death of Jesus on our behalf. Jesus died to deal with the death problem of humanity, a problem that is rooted in the sin problem of humanity (cf. Rom. 6:23). While the concept is not expanded in this context, one should not miss in this passage that Jesus is greater than sin and greater than death.

2:10. There is ambiguity in the pronouns in this verse. Since Jesus is described later in this verse, the first pronoun does not appear to be an antecedent referring to Jesus. Therefore, the earlier pronoun most likely refers to the Father, although the descriptive phrases that follow clearly apply to Jesus as the Father's agent in creation (1:2; cf. John 1:3 and Col. 1:15-17). The point is the same: in order to bring many sons to glory, Jesus as the author of salvation was made perfect through sufferings. Jesus as son is glorified and makes possible the glory of all of God's sons (human creation). Many (v. 10) does not limit the all of v. 9. The terms are used here, as elsewhere, synonymously. The word "author" (*archegos*, leader) is sometimes translated as captain or pioneer and can refer to one who is a trailblazer, cutting a path so others can pass. "Perfect" means complete, mature, equipped for a task, or capable. In the context of

Hebrews, "perfect" does not mean being without sin. This idea of perfection appears in Hebrews three times with reference to Jesus (2:10; 5:9; 7:28).   Jesus was truly human. He was perfected (prepared, equipped, capable), humanly speaking, through suffering (compare 5:8-9).

In the book of Hebrews, perfection, completeness, and maturity are related and are primary themes (cf. 2:10; 5:9, 14; 6:1; 7:11, 19, 28; 9:9, 11; 10:1, 14; 11:40; 12:2, 23).

2:11-13. Understanding the message of this verse (v. 11) depends on understanding the connection between the words "holy" and "sanctified." Literally the verse reads, "the one making holy and those being made holy are all out of one." Jesus sanctifies his followers so that they are holy in Christ and made holy by Christ. The point is confirmed by the fact that Jesus and his followers are one, sometimes translated to say that they are "of the same family and that they are brothers" (even though no word for "family" appears in the original text). The concepts of being brothers and children of God are introduced by the Old Testament quotations in vv. 12-13. This passage is based on the humanity of Jesus described in the context of 2:5-9.

In vv. 12-13 are three Old Testament quotations to describe how Jesus identifies with believers.   Through his suffering, the image of God is restored to human creation. The quotations are all from Messianic passages.

2:12. The quotation is from Ps. 22:22, a chapter that also relates to the crucifixion.

2:13. This verse has quotes from Isa. 8:17 and Isa. 8:18. The point of the quotations is to emphasize Jesus' identity with and unity with believers, a point that will be expanded in the last five verses of the chapter.

2:14-18. The passage begins with a first class condition which is used to state something that is true. Clearly, God's children as a part of human creation are flesh and blood. Jesus shared the same nature and experience. The Word became flesh (John 1:14). Later in the book of Hebrews, this idea is expanded to show that Jesus' participation with humanity also included his temptation, his fervent prayers, and his suffering (5:7-9).

2:14-15. Jesus' participation in the human experience made it possible for him to destroy through his own death the one who had the power of death, the devil. Jesus in overcoming death also overcomes the power of sin and the power of Satan. In this way, by his death, he liberated those who through the fear of death all of their lives were subject to slavery. The idea is that the fear of death enslaved humanity.

2:16. Jesus does not give help to the angels but to the descendants of Abraham, the seed of Abraham, that is, to human beings. This verse continues the argument for the superiority of Jesus over the angels and the superiority of the human creation over the angels (2:5-9).

2:17-18. In order to give such help, it was necessary that Jesus be like his brothers, that he participate in our human nature so he could understand and help (2:11, 18; 4:15; 5:1-3). In doing so, he is qualified to be a merciful and faithful high priest, to make atonement for the sins of the people. These verses introduce the concept that is the primary subject of the book (8:1), a subject that is explained in detail in Chapters 5-10.

In his temptations and sufferings, he understands the human experience and is able to help us in our temptations. Jesus genuinely identifies with the experience of the people of God. The context of vv. 10-18 suggests the following because Jesus participates with and identifies with humanity: (1) recognizing the God who exists, v. 10, (2) reflecting the glory of God, v. 10, (3) being like God, v. 11, (4) praising God, v. 12, (5) trusting God, v. 13, (6) children of the Father, v. 13, (7) sharing human nature, vv. 14-16, and (8) sharing the human experience, v. 18.

Hebrews 3

CONTENT
The paragraphing in this section is included only as a suggestion. The student is encouraged to identify the paragraphs and subsections within the paragraphs as part of his or her personal study. In this chapter, the division of the text into paragraphs is fairly standard in modern translations.

Outline of Chapter
3:1-6, comparison of Jesus and Moses focuses on confessing Jesus with confidence and hope
3:7-11, a rest for the people of God was not attained
3:12-14, second exhortation
3:15-19, explanation of Israel's failure to attain the rest during the wilderness wanderings
Note: the literary unit continues in 4:1-13.

Overview of Chapter
      The literary unit (3:1-4:13) that begins in this chapter compares Jesus to the Old Testament leaders who served under the Mosaic Covenant, specifically mentioning Moses and Joshua. This discussion leads into the long, extended section of the book (5:1-10:18) that deals with details of the Old Testament sacrificial system as it was carried out by the high priest, showing that Jesus as high priest brings a better ministry, a better covenant, and better promises (cf. 8:6).
      The teaching concerning the true rest that God provides depends on a word play between different meanings communicated with the same word. (There are at least four different meanings attached to the concept of "rest" in this section. See comments in Chapter 4.)
      The argument simplified is this: Moses was part of God's household but Jesus was the builder; Moses was a servant while

Jesus was a family member; Moses failed to bring rest but Jesus will not fail.

To enter God's rest, one must be obedient and faithful (the first admonition in 2:1-4 is amplified by the second admonition in 3:12-14).

Because the extended argument of the writer begins in Chapter 3 and continues in Chapter 4 these chapters should be read as a unit.

STUDY HELPS
3:1-6. The book is addressed to "brothers," referring to Jewish believers in Christ. "Brothers" is likely a reference to being brothers in Christ and not to shared Jewish ethnicity. This parallels the references to brothers in 2:12 and 2:17. The recipients of the book are described as partakers of a heavenly calling. In the description of Jesus, two concepts are presented—apostle and high priest. Apostle is not used in an official sense but only in the sense of one who is sent. Hebrews is the only New Testament book that describes Jesus as "apostle" (the Gospel of John speaks of God sending Jesus but does not use the word apostle). "High priest" is repeated from the concluding verses of Chapter 2. To convince first-century Jews that Jesus, from the tribe of Judah, was in fact a priest required an extensive argument which makes up much of the book (5:1-10:18).

The Development of the Message of Hebrews

Chapter 3	Jesus compared to Moses
	Moses was a servant in the house of God
	Under Moses, the people rebelled in disbelief
	Under Moses, the people failed to enter the rest
3:12-14	Second Exhortation: Be Faithful
Chapter 4	The Rest Remains to be Entered
	Jesus compared to Joshua
	Make every effort to enter that rest

These two descriptions show the superiority of Jesus over Moses in the role of God's messenger (Jesus is apostle, one sent) and over Aaron in the role of Levitical high priest (Jesus is a better high priest). For this reason, Jesus is called "the apostle and high priest of our confession." The Christian confession of faith in Christ rests on these two truths. The readers of the book must hold that confession firmly.

3:2-6. Both Moses and Jesus were faithful, but Jesus was worthy of more glory since he was faithful as a son while Moses was faithful as a servant. That Jesus was worthy of more glory than Moses would have been a shocking statement to the Jews.

This text begins with the affirmation that God the Father chose and equipped Jesus for an assigned task and that Jesus was faithful even as all believers are to be faithful. The metaphor of God's people being compared to a house is common in Scripture. In this passage, the phrase is used of a physical building and of a spiritual family. The phrase "testimony of things to be spoken later" refers to the fact that Moses spoke about Jesus. The spiritual house of which the writer speaks is the New Testament family of God. The third class conditional clause in v. 6 states the contingency for believers to be part of this house—if we hold fast our confidence and hope (see 3:6; 6:11; 7:19; 10:23; 11:1). This phrase foreshadows the second warning or admonition in 3:12-14, where part of the phrase is repeated.

3:7-11. Note that these verses, which are a quotation from Ps. 95:7-11, attribute the inspiration of the Old Testament to the Holy Spirit. In the context of Psalm 95, these verses referred to God's warning to Israel in the wilderness against unbelief. The second admonition (3:12-14) and the first part of the exposition concerning true rest (3:15-19) are based on the words of the psalm. The Israelites in the wilderness could have responded to God in faith but instead willfully refused and hardened their hearts in unbelief and disobedience. While God is a God of love, his wrath is equally certain. Both of these characteristics of God should be understood as anthropomorphisms or anthropopathisms, revealing an aspect of God in human terms and emotions. The final phrase, "they shall not enter into my rest," is the key phrase. The point that is developed in Chapters 3-4 centers around the idea of entering God's rest.

Second Exhortation

Watch out, brothers!! Lest there be an evil heart of unbelief that falls away from the living God. But encourage one another every day as long as it is called today, so that no one will be hardened into stubbornness by the deceit of sin. --Hebrews 3:12-13

3:12-14. These verses contain the second exhortation in the book. After describing the unbelief and disobedience of Israel in the wilderness, the author admonishes his readers not to repeat the same mistake. The result of unbelief is departure from God, failing to continue in faith and faithfulness. Deserting God is more often the result of lack of faithfulness than it is the result of lack of faith. Israel in the wilderness had a certain kind of faith but did not act on it and thus became unfaithful. An unbelieving heart will cause one to turn from God. As in 3:1, "brothers" is a reference to other believers rather than to shared Jewish lineage.

TODAY

3:7	Israel	(the original application was to Israel in the desert)
3:7	David	Today if you hear his voice
3:13	The Hebrews	Exhort one another while it is today
3:15	The Hebrews	Today hear his voice and do not harden your hearts
4:7	David	Today....

3:13-19. The goal is faithfulness (as both Moses and Jesus were faithful). One way to guard against unfaithfulness is through mutual, continual encouragement. Problems with unfaithfulness and hard hearts come as a result of sin and its deceitfulness. Refusal and willful unbelief lead to spiritually hard hearts. The mention of "today" in Psalm 95 (cited in 3:7) shows that God's rest was still open in David's time. "Today" in v. 13 repeats that concept for emphasis, pointing out that the time for decision and entering God's rest was still open to the recipients of the book of Hebrews in the first century.

God desired to give Israel rest but they rebelled in the desert. Thus David, about 500 years later, urged Israel to hear God's voice in order to enter his rest. The author of Hebrews takes this to mean that it is still "today" and that the rest is still available (4:1, 6-7). The rest yet remains in the first century, on the basis of what was said through David after the fact.

3:14. We have become participants with Christ only if we hold onto the confidence which we had at the beginning until the end. "If" introduces a third class condition, potential action, indicating that the faithfulness mentioned is not certain. It is possible to begin and not finish. The great need is perseverance; perseverance is the result of faith.

3:15. Here is another third class condition, repeating the quotation from Ps. 95:7-8. The text makes clear that it is possible to miss or reject God's voice. Notice the repetition of the word "today." The opportunity to hear and heed God's voice was still open in the first century. Verse 15 accentuates the warning of v. 12.

3:16-19. Three rhetorical questions focus the point. Who heard and rebelled? Was it not those coming out of Egypt through Moses? With whom was God provoked? The focus on v. 16 is on the fact that the failure of faith occurred under Moses' leadership. Verse 18 provides the contrast between entering God's rest and disobedience to God which is the result of unbelief. The unbelieving Jews were unable to enter the Promised Land after wandering in the wilderness for 40 years because of their unbelief and disobedience.

[Note: Remember that the development of the point being made by the author of Hebrews is not complete at this point and that the literary unit continues in Chapter 4.]

Hebrews 4

[Note: it is suggested that the student read the introductory materials in this guide before beginning individual preparatory reading and analysis.]

CONTENT
The paragraphing included in the Content section of each chapter provides suggestions or guides. The student is encouraged to identify the paragraphs and the subsections within each paragraph to assist in his or her personal study.

The primary paragraphing question in this chapter is whether to connect 4:14-16 with the preceding paragraph or to use it as a bridge and introduction to 5:1-10, as reflected in the outline below.

Outline of Chapter
4:1-11, a rest for the people of God (3:7-4:13)
>   **4:12-13**, God sees and knows hearts
>>   *Note: these verses provide a conclusion to 3:1-4:11 and also provide a bridge to the next literary section.*

4:14-16, Jesus the Great High Priest
Note: the same thought is continued in 5:1-10.

Overview of Chapter
The book of Hebrews is constructed with contrasting sections. For example, the first chapter presents Jesus as Son of God while the second chapter presents Jesus as Son of Man. The third chapter shows that Moses did not lead the people to rest while the fourth chapter asserts that Jesus does lead his people to rest. Inserted in the midst of the contrasting sections are admonitions.

Here is how the construction develops in Chapters 1-2. In Chapter 1 are claims concerning the superiority of Christ to the prophets, the Old Testament revelation, and the angels. These are followed by a word of encouragement to pay attention to the message, to listen and to hold fast (2:1-4). Since Jesus is superior, he and his words must not be rejected. The reason the message about Jesus is so important is explained in Chapter 2 and is summarized in 2:17-18.

In Chapters 3-4, a comparison between Jesus and Moses is developed with these points: the failure of Israel to enter the rest; an admonition not to repeat the same mistake of infidelity and disobedience; since the rest was not attained by Israel, it is yet future as is evident by David's words in Psalm 95; Moses failed to lead the people to rest; Jesus will not fail; God's rest is available to all who will combine the good news with faith.

Using this pattern throughout the book, the message is brought into focus with the admonitions that provide road signs and directions for the reader.

STUDY HELPS

4:1-11. An appropriate response to what is being said is fear. This word is often translated as reverence but here it carries the meaning of being very careful. Because the promise of entering God's rest is still open, one must guard against the danger of not entering that rest. In this chapter are at least four uses of the word rest: (1) in v. 4, God's seventh-day rest after the creation, Gen. 2:2; (2) in v. 8, Joshua's rest in the Promised Land, Num. 13-14; (3) in v. 7, God's rest which was still available in David's day, Ps. 95:7-11; and (4) in v. 9, the ultimate rest with God in heaven.

4:2. "The good news of the gospel was announced to us even as to the Israelites in the wilderness." It was announced to Israel prospectively, but it did not have any impact on them because hearing does not have any value unless there is accompanying faith on the part of those who hear. The unbelieving ones were not permitted to enter the rest in the Promised Land. Of those who left Egypt, only Joshua and Caleb were permitted to enter and that was because of their faith. The Old Testament background of this passage is Numbers 13-14 when the negative report of the spies was accepted by the Israelites and was contradicted only by Joshua and Caleb. The importance of this background passage must not be overlooked. The faith problem related to the spies' report is being repeated by the Hebrew Christians addressed in this book. Faith accepts the word of God and acts accordingly. The first two admonitions are to pay diligent attention to the word of Jesus and to develop faith. The faith that is genuine will be persistent so that faith is synonymous with faithfulness.

4:3. This verse repeats the reference and continues the exposition of Ps. 95:11, expanding what the author has already written about that passage. Only those who believe will enter rest. Therefore, it follows that we who have believed have entered rest just as God intended. This rest seen as parallel to God's rest after his works were finished in the creation of the world. The point is that one does not rest until one's works are finished. For the Israelites, the lack of faith was evidenced by lack of works. They rested too early. They quit too soon. Their faith wavered and disobedience resulted.

4:4. The quotation from Gen. 2:2 is used to support the point just made in v. 3. God did not rest until his works were finished. God's rest on the seventh day makes the connection between the two words "rest" and "seven," a connection that is seen in the word Sabbath, which sometimes means seventh day, sometimes means day of rest, and often means both.

4:5. Combining the quotations from Gen. 2:2 and Ps. 95:11, the writer emphasizes the conclusion stated in Ps. 95:11—they did not enter into God's rest because they did not faithfully complete their work.

4:6-7. Reviewing the argument to this point: some did not enter God's rest, those who first heard the good news about rest did not enter because of disobedience, the quotation from David (Ps. 95:7-11) is repeated in v. 5 because it shows that the rest was still open in David's day. In v. 7, the author repeats the quotation from Ps. 95:11. Note that the passage from Psalm 95 is quoted, at least in part, several times in this section. David spoke of the possibility of entering God's rest long after the events mentioned in Numbers 13-14 and the wilderness wanderings. Disobedience is connected to unfaithfulness because it is the result of lack of faith.

4:8-9. The writer advances the argument. Joshua did not give all of the Israelites the promised rest. Joshua and Jesus are the same name in different forms, probably a play on words even though the Old Testament history is sufficient to make the author's point. If Joshua had given Israel rest, there would not have been the possibility of a reference to God's rest centuries later in the Davidic psalm. David spoke of "today," meaning that the promise of entering remained.

So far in this chapter, the author has (1) declared that the rest is still open, (2) showed that Israel did not enter the rest for lack of faith, (3) set forth God's rest from his labors as the model for rest on the basis of Gen. 2:2, (4) said again that the opportunity was still open in David's day because Joshua did not give them rest, and (5) concluded that the opportunity was still open in the first century in the time of the writing of the book of Hebrews.

4:9-10. Up to this point, the author has used the Greek word *katapausis* to mean rest, but in 4:9 he uses a different word, *sabbatismos*. While these may be used in this context as synonyms with no distinction intended, it is also possible to see a dual application. *Katapausis* refers to the rest that Christians have in Christ when the message is coupled with faith. Some connect this to Matt. 11:28-29 where Jesus invited the weary to come to him for rest. *Sabbatismos* would then refer to eternal rest when one rests from one's labors, even as God rested from his labors after the creation. The next verse (4:11) invites the reader to be diligent to enter into "that rest" (*katapausis*), that is, rest in Christ.

4:10-11. These verses are filled with aorist tenses that signify completed or complete actions. The one who enters rest ceases from his labors, just as God rested on the seventh day. Until one enters the ultimate rest, the believer continues persevering with a faith that is evidenced by actions. Therefore, diligence is required to enter that rest. This does not affirm human merit or performance, but rather eagerness. Such eagerness will keep one from failing into a situation of unfaithfulness and disobedience similar to Israel.

4:12-13. These two verses are one sentence in Greek. Here *logos* refers to God's message. Whatever problems arose in Israel did not come as a result of a faulty word from God. God's message is sufficient and powerful. It has power to penetrate and judge human beings. This affirmation is as much about God's character and faithfulness as it is about specific characteristics of the word of God. God can see and correctly judge faith and faithfulness, or their absence, because everything is open to him (exposed, uncovered). Ultimately, he is the one to whom we must answer. These verses are often read as a threat, but in the context, they have also a comforting aspect. Jesus understands our humanity. God will make just judgments.

4:14-16. These verses introduce an extended section of text that continues through 10:18. The paragraph that begins here extends through 5:10. The passage picks up the description of Jesus as a great high priest (cf. 2:17-18, 3:1). After the warning against disbelief and disobedience (3:7-4:13), the author returns to the theme of Jesus as High Priest. The pattern mentioned above, that admonitions are inserted in the midst of teaching sections, is repeated with the warning in 5:11-14 inserted into the extended description of Jesus' high priestly function (Chapters 5-10).

We as readers two millennia removed from the historical context may not have problems in accepting the message of Hebrews. The first-century Jews to whom the book was addressed would have struggled mightily with this comparison of the old covenant and the new covenant, and even more with the idea of Jesus as a priest from a tribe other than Levi. In the Old Testament, the Messiah is described as a priest only in Psalm 110 and Zechariah 4. Jesus, our high priest, has passed through the heavens to appear in the presence of the Father. This fact in and of itself is sufficient motivation to hold fast the confession of our faith (let us persevere in faith). Jesus is described as the Son of God, reminding the readers of what has already been presented in Chapters 1-2.

4:15. Even though he is Son of God, Jesus as our high priest can sympathize with our weakness, a point that was introduced in 2:5-18. Jesus never yielded to sin even though he was tempted just as we are. This verse does not mean that Jesus experienced every possible temptation, but that he knew the true nature of temptation in his existence as a human being. Jesus understands our situation.

4:16. Therefore, we can draw near with confidence to the throne of grace. "Draw near" will be repeated several times in the book. The point, which will be expanded in the following chapters, is that we can approach God through the sacrifice of

Jesus (7:25; 10:1, 22; 11:6). In the context, the throne of grace refers to God's presence. Drawing near to God, we receive mercy and grace sufficient to meet our needs.

Hebrews 5

[Note: it is suggested that the student read the introductory materials in this guide before beginning individual preparatory reading and analysis.]

CONTENT
The paragraphing included in the Content section of each chapter provides suggestions or guides for reading based on the topics presented. The student is encouraged to identify the paragraphs and the subsections within each paragraph as part of his or her personal study. In this chapter, the division of the text into paragraphs is the same in most modern translations. After the paragraphs are identified, the student should try to summarize the content of each section in a short phrase.

Outline of Chapter
5:1-10, Jesus the Great High Priest
5:11-14, warning against spiritual immaturity and failing to understand the faith of Jesus
Note: the larger literary unit continues through 6:12; some would continue it through 6:20.

Overview of Chapter
     Of the two descriptions of Jesus in 3:1-6 (apostle and high priest), the book of Hebrews develops the latter (cf. 2:17; 3:1; 4:14-15; 5:5, 10; 6:20; 7:26, 28; 8:1, 3; 9:11; 10:21).
     The priesthood of Jesus according to the order of Melchizedek is not an easy concept to understand. The literary unit in 5:11-6:20 is inserted into the discussion about Melchizedek. Notice how smoothly the text flows if one goes directly from 5:10 to 7:1 in the reading.
     The literary section in 5:11-6:20 is introduced with the third warning or admonition of the book.
     The pronouns used in 5:11-6:12 will help guide our understanding of this passage: you, we, they, you.

STUDY HELPS

5:1-4. This short introductory paragraph summarizes the Old Testament high priestly system. High priests were human beings who were appointed to stand before God on behalf of other human beings; priests were chosen from the tribe of Levi; high priests offered gifts and sacrifices for sins; high priests were compassionate with others because they were also sinners; high priests offered sacrifices for themselves before offering sacrifices for the sins of the people; high priests were chosen by God and could not apply, volunteer, or advance themselves as candidates.

The Development of the Message of Hebrews

4:14-16	Jesus the Great High Priest
Chapter 5	Jesus the Great High Priest
	Chosen by God as a "Melchizedek High Priest"
5:11-6:20	Third Exhortation: Maturity, Grow Up
	Excursus: God's promise and oath
Chapter 7	A "Melchizedek High Priest"
8:1-6	"This is the point...."

5:2. In the Old Testament, sins of ignorance and misunderstanding were forgivable, intentional premeditated sin was not (see Num. 15:22-31). This point is an important part of the author's development of the theme (compare 10:26-31), especially if some of the Jewish Christians were intentionally leaving Christ, returning to Judaism, or compromising the uniqueness of Christianity by attempting to mix it with Judaism.

5:3. The high priest offered sacrifices for his own sins before offering sacrifices for the sins of the people (Lev. 9:7-17). A contrast to this point is presented in 7:26, 27 where it is noted that Jesus did not have to make an offering for himself.

5:4. The high priestly office was only by God's appointment of certain people from a certain tribe and a certain family.

5:5-10. This section shows how the high priestly service of Christ corresponds to the Old Testament system. The author begins the task of convincing first-century Jews that Christ can serve as high priest.

Christ did not glorify himself to make himself a high priest. God is the one who made the choice, a fact made clear by citations from Ps. 2:7 (see Heb. 1:5 where the same verse is cited) and Ps. 110:4. Psalm 110 is Messianic and uniquely gives the Messiah both priestly and royal offices. The development of the Melchizedek connection is interrupted by the insertion of 5:11-6:20 (compare 5:10 and 7:1). The narrative about Melchizedek and Abraham is found in Gen. 14:17-20. The primary point in 5:5-10 is that God is the one who selected Jesus to serve as a high priest.

5:7. The comparison of Jesus as high priest with the Old Testament system priestly continues. This verse refers to Jesus during his earthly sojourn and ministry when he prayed earnestly in Gethsemane. He prayed to the One who could save him from death. This text says he was heard even though he was not spared the agony of the cross. He died but was resurrected from death. The last word in the verse is variously translated: he was heard because of his fear (submission, humility, piety, devotion).

5:8-9. Being a son, he learned obedience through the things he suffered. Recall that a primary point of the author has been that Jesus is a son. As a son, yet human, he was tempted, he prayed, he cried, he suffered, he learned submission (obedience). He was faithful to God's purpose and thus obedient (in contrast to those in the wilderness who were unbelieving and disobedient). The point is clear: Jesus suffered on our behalf and thus learned obedience; when we are called upon to suffer, we should also respond with obedience. Jesus is son of God, but he is capable of understanding us because of what he experienced in his life on this earth as a human being.

These verses present the difficult challenge of how to understand Jesus' deity and Jesus' humanity. How can Jesus as deity be obedient? How can Jesus as deity be made perfect? These statements must have to do with his human experience. He was made the perfect high priest, the perfect sacrifice, the ideal of humanity capable of understanding our human situation. Jesus is the source of salvation only for those who are obedient.

Note again that perfection and maturity are related concepts that serve as principal themes in Hebrews (cf. 2:10; 5:9, 14; 6:1; 7:11, 19, 28; 9:9, 11; 10:1, 14; 11:40; 12:2, 23).

5:10. All of what has been said about Jesus as high priest hinges on his designation by God as a high priest according to the order of Melchizedek. Melchizedek is an important model because he is called both priest and king. This theme will be continued in 7:1 after the insertion of 5:11-6:20.

Third Exhortation

Concerning this we have much to say, and it is hard to explain since you have become dull and sluggish of hearing. For even when by this time you should be teachers, you need to be taught the beginning principles of God's message, you have an appetite for milk and not solid food. Everyone who needs milk is incapable in the word of righteousness, being immature. Solid food is for the mature who through constant practice have exercised their perceptions to discern good and evil. --Hebrews 5:11-14

5:11-14. The next literary unit begins in 5:11 and extends through 6:12. If the literary unit is understood as including 5:11-6:20, there are subunits in 5:11-6:12 and 6:13-20. The careful student has likely noted by now that the development of the arguments by the author of Hebrews at times does not follow the chapter and verse divisions that were added later.

5:11. Concerning "him"—the reference can be to either Jesus or Melchizedek, but in the context, a reference to Jesus as high priest is more likely—there is much to be said. These are difficult matters, but before going further, one of the problems of the recipients must be addressed. "You have become hard of hearing and lazy spiritually."

Notice the change in pronouns: we or us (5:11; 6:1-3, 9), you (5:11, 12; 6:9-12), and they (6:4-8). These internal markers will be helpful in understanding the development of the author's thought in this passage.

5:12. You should be able to teach others due to the time you have spent as Christians, but you have not matured in faith. In fact, you are in need of teaching, and the teaching you need is not advanced teaching but rather the very basic, elementary, foundational truths of God's revelation. The writer calls these milk and not solid food, accentuating the immaturity of the readers. Length of time spent in Christianity is not directly related to maturity. Some Christian mature very rapidly; others seem never to reach maturity.

5:13-14. Those who need milk are unable to digest the word of righteousness because they are spiritual infants. Those who are capable of digesting solid food are mature and have learned how to discern good and evil. Mature is from the same root as perfect in 5:9.

Hebrews 6

[Note: it is suggested that the student read the introductory materials in this guide before beginning individual preparatory reading and analysis.]

CONTENT
The outlining and paragraphing included in the Content section of each chapter provide suggestions. The student is encouraged to identify the paragraphs and the subsections within each paragraph in his or her personal study. The division of the text into paragraphs is fairly standard in modern translations. In this chapter, identifying the smaller sections within the paragraph, as in the outline below, will help one understand the message.

Outline of Chapter
5:11-6:12, warning against abandoning the faith
5:11-14, the problem of immaturity among the recipients of the book
6:1-3, the commitment of Christians is to go forward
6:4-6, the problem of not progressing, illustrated in the experience of a group who have reached the point of no return
6:7-8, a parable
6:9-12, a better expectation concerning the recipients gives hope and encouragement
6:13-20, God's sure promise (excursus)

Overview of Chapter
There are various theories about the recipients of the book, including the idea that two groups of Jews are being addressed—believers and unbelievers. Some have advanced this idea in an effort to explain the passage in 5:11-6:12. That the author is writing to unbelievers is unlikely, and such is not necessary to explain the passage. The message of this section goes something like this: here is your problem (5:11-14), here is how we Christians handle the problem (6:1-3), some in a similar situation have gone so far that they cannot recover (6:4-6), it is sad when land that receives God's blessings does not bear fruit (6:7-8),

because we do not believe you are beyond recovery we have a higher expectation concerning you (6:9-12).

The admonition (5:11-14) included in this section (5:11-6:12) is related to the previous admonitions. The common message is to beware of the problem of disbelief—as seen in failing to pay attention to the message, willful unbelief, and spiritual immaturity.

When one understands 6:4-8 in its context and notes the changes in the pronouns, the passage is not difficult to understand.

Problems related to faith are never easy, but it should be clear that some Christians begin well and finish poorly. Believers can so live as to be unfit for Christian service. The Bible is filled with examples of carnal Christians, immature Christians, disqualified Christians, unfruitful Christians, artificial results, false professions, false teachers, and those who fall away after beginning.

The paragraph in 6:13-20 uses the mention of the promises at the end of v. 12 as a springboard to explain the importance of God's promises. The promise to Abraham was confirmed by God's word and by God's oath. Because God cannot lie, God's word is sufficient surety. The oath makes doubly certain the unchangeable nature of God's promise. These same ideas are applied to Jesus' high priesthood in Chapter 7. Here they are used to point to Jesus as our forerunner who enters God's presence as our high priest, according to the order of Melchizedek.

STUDY HELPS

6:1-3. These verses continue the inserted literary unit that began in 5:11. In 5:12 the author observes that the recipients ("you") need to be taught again the elements (*stoichia*) of the beginning (*arche*) of the oracles (*logion*). *Stoicheion* refers to any fundamental or first thing, thus first principles or elements. The verb form means to proceed in a row or go in order. The recipients of the book have somehow missed the basics and are therefore incapable of continuing the growth process. In 6:1, a similar concept is described: "having left the teaching (*logos*) of the beginning (*arche*)...." "Beginning" (*arche*) is another word that refers to elementary teachings or first principles. In the context, *arche* (beginning) is the opposite of *teleios* (ending, maturity). The comparison of 5:12 and 6:1-2 makes the efforts to identify different recipients, situations, or purposes in these verses unconvincing. Notice also that the repeated reference to maturity (5:14; 6:1).

The recipients need to move beyond (leave) the basics and move toward maturity. "We" Christians are characterized by spiritual growth and maturity. Maturity does not come by returning to and focusing on those matters that are easy, matters about which agreement is common. In the context, it may be that the items mentioned—repentance, faith, washings, laying on of hands, resurrection and judgment—are Christian subjects shared with Judaism. Regardless, leaving the elementary teaching about Christ means moving forward, not backward. The things mentioned are important, but they are not the matters that characterize spiritual maturity. They are basic teachings. (These subjects are not treated in detail in this study guide since many commentaries define the words and outline the difficulties and possible applications.)

The meaning of the text is this: the call to leave the elementary teachings about Christ and move toward maturity is not answered by returning to Judaism or by returning to the teachings that are shared by Christianity and Judaism. Maturity means moving forward in faith in Christ. Maturity is the commitment of "we" who are Christians.

6:3. "This we will do." The verse contains a third class condition, but the potential action described (if God permit) seems certain. This phrase, "If God permit," has an interesting use of this grammatical construction since the third-class condition usually indicates contingency, something that may or may not be possible.

6:4-8. This section of the text describes how some have begun and afterward fallen away, resulting in the impossibility of restoration or renewal to repentance. In the context, the message is that some others have been lost by going down the path that some of the recipients were contemplating.

These verses comprise the "they" or "those" section of the text. They (not the recipients of the book, but another group) had understood, had enjoyed the benefits, had been partakers of the Holy Spirit, had known God's good word and had seen the powerful promises of the future. Afterward they had fallen away. These are aorist participles—descriptions of the past reality. They had known God. There is no contextual reason to doubt their full faith in Christ since nothing in the text suggests that there was a problem in their faith. The idea that the writer uses a hypothetical situation to motivate the readers is not demanded by the textual construction.

In v. 6b begins a series of present tense verbs. It is impossible to renew "them" to repentance. This verse has the first of four uses of the concept of impossibility in Hebrews (6:4, 6:18, 10:4, 11:6). One reason for the inability to renew them is that they crucify to themselves the Son of God and put Him to open shame (see Matt. 1:19 for a parallel reference to open shame). Note the intensified form of crucify (seen in the prefix, *ana*)—they crucify to themselves or they crucify again.

6:7-8. The illustration relates to the verses immediately above. Many references to cultivation and crops can be found in the Bible, for example in Jesus' parables. Those who receive God's good gifts (6:4) should yield fruit so they can be blessed even more. If the product is not fruit but is rather thorns and thistles, the ultimate result is destruction. The application in the context is this: how incredible is it to think that some would enjoy God's good blessings and have the possibility of bearing fruit, and afterward reject God so that the only result is thorns and thistles.

6:9-12. Even though the recipients were immature (5:11-14) and needed to move forward in the faith (6:1-3), they were not as far gone as those described in 6:4-8. The author seeks to encourage his readers—we believe better things concerning you, things of salvation and blessing (rather than destruction).

6:9. "We are convinced of better things concerning you, things that accompany salvation." The emphasis on "better" appears throughout the book. "Things of salvation" speaks of those things belonging in a certain group. The things expected are not described, but one can develop a list of possible applications by considering the things mentioned in this context as well as those in the wider context of the book.

6:10-12. This confidence on the part of the author is based on God's justice, and the work and love the recipients have demonstrated previously. God is a just judge (cf. 12:23). As they have been diligent in ministering to other Christians, they are admonished to use the same diligence and perseverance with regard to their faithfulness to Christ. Three results are mentioned: in this way (1) they will reach the goal with full assurance, (2) they will not become dull (cf. 5:11), a word that contrasts with diligence, and (3) they will be imitators of those who inherit the promises through faith and patience. This last phrase refers to Old Testament believers who continued faithfully in the midst of great difficulties (compare those who were unfaithful in Chapter 3 with those who were faithful in Chapter 11). "The promises of God" provides a point of transition for the next paragraph (6:13-20).

6:13-20. Perhaps the best way to describe this section is as an excursus. It is only indirectly related to what has come before, but it anticipates what is yet to come and provides foundations for the argument to be made by the writer.

God's promises are dependable because God is faithful. One who understands God's faithfulness will continue with faith and patience, looking forward in hope. The writer turns to the Abraham story to illustrate this point. God promised that Abraham would be blessed and that his descendants would be multiplied. According to 6:15, Abraham believed the promise in full assurance of faith and waited patiently (cf. Romans 4). Considering the development of the argument in Hebrews, the choice of this illustration was likely intentional, considering that the promise to Abraham preceded the coming of the Old Testament law and Levitical system. When God made this promise, he "swore by himself" so that the promise depended only on God's unchanging character (God cannot lie) and his unchanging purpose.

6:16. Oaths serve to confirm agreements and commitments, and are used to end disputes about what was agreed to. In the same way (6:17), God used an oath to confirm to the heirs of the promise his unchanging commitment and purpose.

6:18. The phrase "two unchangeable things" refers to God's oath and God's promise. Since God cannot lie, both the oath and the promise are dependable. God's word is our assurance so that Christians (we who have taken refuge in Christ) are encouraged to continue forward to reach the hope that is before us. Human beings are called to respond to the trustworthy God. This response involves faith until the end.

6:19-20. The Christian hope is like an anchor to the soul, indicating immovability, safety, and security. The anchor is steadfast (*asfales*, unfailing, certain, safe, confirming, true) and firm (*bebaios*, stable, trustworthy). This hope "reaches behind the curtain." This refers to entering the Most Holy Place, referring to Jesus as our great high priest. The high priest entered the Holy of Holies where the furniture symbolized the very presence of God. So also, Jesus our high priest enters the heavenly tabernacle and the very presence of God (8:5, 9:23). Jesus' entry to God's presence makes him our forerunner (*prodromos*) and guarantees our presence with God.

"Forerunner" is a scout that determines the correct path, a pioneer, or a ship that leads a larger ship to port. The Christian hope is based on God's oath and thus on God's character, on God's promises that are consistent with his eternal purpose. Jesus as our high priest, an eternal high priest according to the order of Melchizedek, fulfills God's promise. Jesus' entry to the presence of God as our high priest is the foundation of our hope. The importance of Jesus' high priesthood, with a better ministry, better covenant, and better promises, as the way to receive God's promises is the subject of Chapters 7-12.

Hebrews 7

[Note: it is suggested that the student read the introductory materials in this guide before beginning individual preparatory reading and analysis.]

CONTENT

The paragraphing included in this Content section is intended only to give suggestions. The student is encouraged to identify the paragraphs and the subsections within each paragraph. This will be of much help in his or her personal study. The task of personal reading and analysis is essential, even though the division of the text into paragraphs is usually fairly standard in translations.

Outline of Chapter

7:1-3, the story of Melchizedek as a priest receiving tithes from Abraham
7:4-10, what it means that Abraham pays tithes to Melchizedek
7:11-21, this demonstrates the need for a new priesthood and the replacement of the Law
7:22-28, the greatness and perfection of Christ's unchanging, heavenly priesthood
[Note: Some modern translations put a paragraph break after v. 19, but in the context, it seems better to put vv. 20-21 with the preceding paragraph and begin the new thought at v. 22.]

Overview of Chapter

The text in 7:1 resumes the thought from 5:10, following the third warning and the explanation concerning the promise to Abraham that were inserted in 5:11-6:20. A major focus in the rest of the book is that the promise to Abraham, ultimately fulfilled in Jesus, is the foundation for the better promises available to the readers.

The outline above summarizes well the content of the chapter. The author sets forth the justification for Christ's high priesthood, the necessity of replacing the previous covenant, and the superiority of Christ's high priesthood.

STUDY HELPS

7:1-3. Melchizedek was a king and priest in Salem (later called Jerusalem) during the time of Abraham. The historical account is in Gen. 14:18-20. The only other biblical text that mentions him is Ps. 110:4. He is referred to as a "priest of the Most High God." In the context, he is used to illustrate Jesus' high priesthood for at least the following reasons. (1) He was a priest of the Most High God. (2) Abraham gave him tithes, indicating the superiority of Melchizedek to Abraham (the lesser gives tithes to the greater) and to Levi who figuratively gave tithes to Melchizedek (vv. 4-9). (3) He does not have a priestly lineage so a divine priesthood is established apart from the Old Testament sacrificial system. (4) He combines the figures of priest and king, the only Old Testament person to do so (see Psalm 110 for the use of this point referring to the Messiah). (5) In continuing as a priest forever, he resembles the Son of God.

Melchizedek blessed Abraham. The greater blesses the lesser, demonstrating superiority over Abraham. Figuratively Levi was blessed by Melchizedek which shows that Melchizedek is superior as a priest over the Aaronic priesthood (Aaron being a descendant of Levi). Since Melchizedek was a priest apart from the Old Testament system, Jesus can also be a priest of a different order, even though he is from a different tribe and not from the tribe of Levi.

7:2. Abraham gave to Melchizedek a tithe of the spoils. The concept of the tithe predates the Mosaic Law, as does the Sabbath. Melchizedek's name, King of Righteousness, and his title, King of Salem (which means King of Peace), demonstrate a direct connection with the Messiah who will usher in a time of righteousness and peace.

7:3. This verse uses rabbinical hermeneutics to show that since the lineage of Melchizedek is not given, nor details of his birth or death, his eternal priesthood resembles the Son of God who is eternal Messiah. His priesthood is eternal. He is like the Son of God. This comparison is primary in this chapter. Of course, Melchizedek had parents and a lineage, but the point is that they are not named in the biblical text.

7:4-10. Having set forth the important details of the Melchizedek story, the author moves to his point. Here is a summary: The greatness of Melchizedek has been demonstrated by the fact that Abraham gave him tithes before the Law came. Under the Law, it was the priests, mortal men, who received a tithe from the people and they (the priests) were Abraham's descendants. Abraham paid tithes to one who was not in the line of descent, to one who yet "lives." In addition, Abraham was blessed by Melchizedek. Therefore, it can be said that Levi, the one who later received tithes, paid tithes to Melchizedek. This depends on rabbinic logic about Levi being present in the loins of Abraham (v. 10).

7:6-7. Since the one who does not have a priestly genealogy collected a tithe from Abraham and blessed Abraham, and since the lesser is blessed by the greater, the conclusion must be that Melchizedek was greater.

This continues the theme of greater (better, superior, more excellent) that recurs in the book (1:4; 6:9; 7:7; 7:19, 22; 8:6; 9:23; 10:34; 11:16, 35, 40; 12:24). The theme of the book is that Jesus' high priesthood is better than the high priestly system upon which the law was based. From this idea will be developed the necessity of a new covenant, that the new covenant of Christ is better than the old covenant, and that it leads to better promises.

7:8-10. The argument the author is presenting turns on the eternal nature of Melchizedek's priesthood—eternal because his genealogy, parentage, and death are not recorded and because Ps. 110:4 refers to his priesthood as "forever." The mortal man, Melchizedek, who received tithes thus "lives on." And Levi who received tithes under the old covenant paid tithes figuratively through Abraham. By extension, the Jewish priests, even the high priests, paid tithes to Melchizedek, making him the greater. Therefore, Jesus' high priesthood after the order of Melchizedek is a greater priesthood, superior to the Jewish priesthood.

7:11-22. In this paragraph, the author continues the development of his point, connecting the Levitical priesthood and the Law, showing that if the Levitical priesthood is being replaced, the Law must also be replaced. The verb that is often translated change means "to put in place of." "Replace" better represents the original meaning than "change." What is the message of these verses? These verses say exactly the opposite of what is often taught. Note carefully what the text says. When the Levitical priesthood was replaced by Jesus' high priesthood, this necessitated a replacement of the Old Testament Law that was received under the Old Testament priesthood.

7:11-12. The Greek second class conditional clause indicates that the statement is not true. Perfection was not possible through the Levitical priestly system and the law. "Perfection" is from the same word family as maturity. In the context, perfection refers to the complete forgiveness of sins by the perfect sacrifice, but also recalls the lack of maturity mentioned in 5:11-6:3. That the Law came through the Levitical system may refer to Moses who as giver of the Law was from the tribe of Levi. The statement could also reflect the fact that one task of the priests was to teach the Law. The connection would normally be stated in reverse, that the priestly system was based on the teachings of the Law.

The imperfection of the priestly system shows the imperfection of the Law and demonstrates the need for another priest, not according to the Aaronic order, but according to a better or greater order, which the order of Melchizedek is, as explained in the previous verses. The change in the priestly system necessitated a change in the law, that is, considering the context of Hebrews, the introduction of a new covenant. Again, the word translated "change" is better understood as "replacement."

7:13-14. The coming of a new priestly order and the new covenant would involve "one from another tribe" from which altar officiants were not chosen under the Levitical system and the Law. Jesus came from the tribe of Judah. Moses and the old Law never spoke of priests coming from this tribe. Judah was the forefather of the Davidic royal lineage but was never part of a priestly lineage in the Old Testament.

7:15-17. With the first class conditional clause, the first part of the sentence is considered to be true. Such phrases are often translated in English with the word "since." Since another priest has arisen from the lineage or order of Melchizedek, the argument is valid. Such a priest does not serve on the basis of a law that looked at physical requirements or fleshly command-ments, that is through physical descent; such a priest serves on the basis of an indestructible life. The argument, following rab-binic style, is this: because Melchizedek's parents and lineage are not given, and because his priesthood was "forever" accord-ing to Ps. 110:4, Melchizedek's life and priesthood continue (also see v. 21). This statement is applied by extension to Jesus who has the endless life of God so that he is a priest forever ac-cording to the Messianic psalm (110). This application is based on the oath and promise of God, pointing back to 6:13-20, and thus is certain and unchangeable.

7:18-22. The previous commandment (the law, specifi-cally the law related to high priests) is set aside or annulled because it was defective and has become weak and useless (8:13). The idea of setting aside a commandment of God was likely as difficult to accept for the Jews as it would be for us today if one were to appear and claim that a certain part of the New Testament is to be set aside. We perhaps do not appreciate the mental conflict that this biblical teaching presented to the Jews (compare passages such as Matt. 5:17-19, Galatians 3, Romans 2, and Ephesians 2).

7:19-21. The law made nothing perfect. The Old Testa-ment law could not bring people to God. The new system with Jesus the high priest makes possible a better hope so we can draw near to God (4:16; 7:25; 10:1, 19-22). This new system was con-firmed with an oath of God (Ps. 110:4, quoted here in vv. 21-22) and is backed by God's character (6:13-17). It is thus immuta-ble.

7:22. Jesus is the guarantee or pledge of a better covenant. This better covenant, introduced here, will be the subject of the next section of the book (8:1-10:18).

7:23-28. These verses present another comparison of Jesus and the Old Testament priests, apparently included with the goal of finalizing the argument. Christ's priesthood is great, unchanging, heavenly, and perfect.

7:23-25. In comparison to the eternal priesthood pre-sented in the previous verses, the Old Testament priests were human beings who died. Therefore, it was necessary to have multiple high priests through the years. Jesus continues forever as a permanent high priest. This idea again refers back to Melchizedek's lack of lineage and the "forever" priesthood described in Ps. 110:4. Jesus is always available to save, and to save completely, those who draw near to God through him. He lives forever to make intercession, fulfilling the role of high priest. Redemption through Jesus was made possible through the cross and continues as he presents the case of the believers before the throne (4:15-16; 9:23-28).

7:26-28. Some think these verses contain a quotation from an early hymn. Jesus comes as a different type of high priest—holy, innocent, sinless, undefiled and thus the perfect sacrifice, separated from human beings (with regard to sin), and exalted (preeminent). His sacrifice is not continual as was the case under the Old Testament. The contrast is seen in that he made one sacrifice, once and for all, when he sacrificed himself.

The Law appointed weak human beings as priests, but the oath (referring to God's word in Ps. 110:4) which came after the law in point of time, appoints as high priest a Son who is forever made perfect (2:10; 5:8-9). The idea of the "Son" builds on the theme that was developed in Chapters 1-3. The royal lineage made sons into kings. Now the "Son" is also capable of fulfilling the priestly function.

Hebrews 8

[Note: it is suggested that the student read the introductory materials in this guide before beginning individual preparatory reading and analysis.]

CONTENT

The paragraphing included in the Content section of each chapter provides suggestions and guidance. The student is encouraged to identify the paragraphs as part of his or her personal study and analysis of the biblical text. The division of the text into paragraphs is fairly standard in this chapter.

Outline of Chapter

8:1-6, Jesus the high priest, in the heavenly sanctuary

8:6, Jesus has a better ministry, brings a new and better covenant, with better promises

8:7-13, the new covenant was promised in the Old Testament; the old covenant was defective

Overview of Chapter

This chapter is part of a much longer extended context (5:1-10:18). Chapters 5-7 give details of the author's first point: the high priesthood of Jesus. A parenthetical section (5:12-6:20) contains the third exhortation of the book and an excursus concerning God's faithfulness in fulfilling his promises. In Chapter 8 begins a section that will explain in more detail the need for a change of the covenant based on the change of the priesthood (8:7-10:18).

The book of Hebrews frequently uses Old Testament citations and develops its arguments based on those Old Testament texts. In Chapter 1, seven Old Testament citations were used to support the point that Jesus is superior to the angels. Chapter 2 was developed around Psalm 8. Chapter 3-4 were developed on the basis of Ps. 95:7-11. Chapters 5-7 were developed around Ps. 110. This chapter will develop Jeremiah 31, with the quotation from Jeremiah 31 repeated in 10:16-18. The passage in 8:1-10:18 is one extended literary unit and develops one primary theme.

In 8:1, the author identifies the main point of the book: we have such a high priest. In 8:6, one can trace the development of the argument presented by the writer of Hebrews. Jesus has obtained a more excellent ministry (high priesthood). This was explained in Chapters 5-7. This change in the priesthood necessitates a change of covenant, and by his priesthood Jesus is the mediator of a better covenant. The change in the covenant is the subject of 8:1-10:18. This better covenant has been enacted based on better promises. The theme of God's promises was introduced in the excursus of 6:12-20, and will be expanded in the section beginning in 10:19 through the end of Chapter 12.

STUDY HELPS
8:1-6. The author gives a summary of the book to this point (vv. 1-2): we have a high priest like the one just described—forever, after the order of Melchizedek, now seated at the right hand of the throne in heaven, a minister in the true tabernacle and the true sanctuary made by God. The author will say more about the themes of the new covenant and the heavenly sanctuary in Chapters 8-10. Jesus' better ministry and sacrifice require a new covenant.

In Hebrews Jesus is described as a high priest who ushers in a new covenant. No other New Testament book uses this figure of high priest to describe Jesus. The priestly function of Jesus is seen in Psalm 110 and was revealed also in the prophets. Jesus is both king and priest. Continuing the explanation of Psalm 110, the writer describes Jesus as seated at the right hand of the Majesty on high. This signifies royalty—the figure is not used of priests. It also communicates authority. The Majesty on high is God—remember the hesitancy of the Jews to use God's name.

The Development of the Message of Hebrews

4:14-7:28	A Better Ministry
8:1-6	"This is the point...."
8:7-10:18	A Better Covenant

8:2. Here is continued the development of the idea of the celestial tabernacle and sanctuary (Holy of Holies, presence of God) that was mentioned briefly in 6:19-20. The text mentions a tabernacle in heaven. The tabernacle that was revealed to Moses in Sinai and constructed during the wilderness wanderings was only a copy of the original in heaven (9:11, 24). The original was erected by God (cf. 11:10), not by human beings. The copy in the wilderness was erected by human beings. Jesus is a minister in the authentic, celestial tabernacle and serves as high priest in the celestial sanctuary.

8:3-4. Since high priests offer gifts and sacrifices, it was necessary that Jesus as high priest offer a sacrifice. The reference is to Jesus' sacrificial death on the cross. If Jesus were still on earth, he would not be a priest and he would not need to make the offerings that were required by the Law because there were others responsible for that task. Jesus' high priestly work occurs in the context of the celestial sanctuary.

8:5-6. The activities of the Levitical priests on earth occurred in a tabernacle that is a copy and shadow of the celestial. The writer proves this point by reminding his readers that Moses was warned by God to do everything according to the pattern received on the mountain. The pattern given to Moses was a copy based on the celestial sanctuary of God's presence (Ex. 25:9, 40; the Old Testament quotation is from Ex. 25:40).

The ministry of Jesus in the true sanctuary is more excellent; he is mediator (cf. 9:15; 12:24) of a better covenant based on better promises. Here the emphasis on "better" is repeated. The verbs are all in the perfect tense indicating that all this has been accomplished. This verse (8:6) provides a good outline of Chapters 5-12: Jesus' high priesthood (5-7), the better covenant (8:1-10:18), the better promises (10:19-12:29).

8:7-13. A second class conditional clause, contrary to fact, introduces the second section of the chapter. The first covenant was not faultless. The defects in the first covenant gave rise to the second. The first covenant could not meet the need of humanity for restoration of relationship with God and righteous faithful living. The law could not answer the problem of human weakness. The first covenant could not cleanse the conscience of the worshiper. The defects of the first covenant are the primary emphasis of this part of the book (8:7-10:18).

8:8-9. The writer supports the claim of 8:6-7 with a quotation from Jer. 31:31-34 (cited in 8:8-12). The same verses are cited again at the conclusion of the section (10:15-18). Jeremiah 31 is the only text in the Old Testament which speaks of the new covenant, although the description in Ezek. 36:22-28 relates to the coming of this new relationship with God. Note the reuniting of Israel and Judah under the new covenant. The new covenant will not be like the former covenant, established with God's people as they were leaving Egypt. Israel did not honor and keep the first covenant; they did not continue faithfully in the former covenant and this displeased God.

8:10-12. The new covenant will be personal—I will be their God and they will be my people; the phrase uses an Old Testament covenantal formula. The new covenant will be written not on stone but in minds and hearts. (See the book of Deuteronomy for an extended Old Testament focus on the importance of the heart in maintaining relationship with God.)

8:11-12. In the Old Testament system Jews became participants in the covenant through physical birth. Therefore, it was necessary to teach people to know the Lord, even though they were already included in the covenant. Under the new covenant, that will not be necessary, for the only ones who are included in the new covenant are those who have already come to know the Lord. Every person who draws nears to God under the new covenant—on the basis of the high priesthood of Jesus—will know the Lord, without respect of persons. In this way, God will demonstrate mercy and deal with sin once and for all. "I will remember their sins no more."

8:13. The reference to a new covenant (Jer. 31:31-34) makes clear that God's intention to establish another covenant goes back centuries. Now that the first covenant is not needed and is obsolete, it is "old" and is about to disappear. It is impossible to cling to the Old Law because it is no longer in effect and is gone. One cannot go back to that which no longer exists. The Old Testament law had a purpose (Gal. 3:16-24), but when that purpose was fulfilled, the law was no longer needed.

Hebrews 9

[Note: it is suggested that the student read the introductory materials in this guide before beginning individual preparatory reading and analysis.]

CONTENT

The chapter outlines in the Content section for each chapter are the result of my own study and are only suggestions or guides. The student should identify the paragraphs and the subsections within each paragraph as part of her or his own personal study. The division of the text into paragraphs is fairly standard in modern translations. Identifying the paragraphing of the text is helpful in reading, analysis, and understanding.

<u>Outline of Chapter</u>
9:1-5, the earthly sanctuary
9:6-10, limitations of the earthly sanctuary
9:11-14, the heavenly sanctuary, introducing an explanation of the sacrifice of Christ
9:15-22, the death of the testator or mediator seals the new covenant with blood
9:23-28, Christ's great work as mediator and sacrifice takes away sin permanently, providing access to God
Note: this chapter leads to a summary explanation of Christ's work as high priest in 10:1-18, where the literary section concludes.

<u>Overview of Chapter</u>
The author begins the chapter with a detailed description of some of the aspects of priestly system in the Old Testament but soon concludes that time does not allow more detail. The purpose of this description is to show the limitations of the previous priesthood, especially with the need for continual sacrifice and the lack of continual access to God's presence. Against this backdrop, the author shows how the new priesthood based on the sacrifice of Christ is better. Jesus inaugurated the new covenant or testament by the shedding of his blood (just as purification under the previous testament required blood). The new covenant is better because the sacrifice of Christ takes away sin

permanently and because Christ the mediator gives continual access to God's throne room.

STUDY HELPS

9:1-5. In this paragraph is a description of various regulations and details of the tabernacle and the Holy of Holies under the first covenant (the Old Testament). These are also described in Leviticus. The word "covenant" is not in the original text. It is included in the translations for clarity because the word "first" refers to the first covenant. Most often in the Bible, the tabernacle refers to the portable structure that was used for worship in the wilderness (see Exodus 25-40). In the context of 9:1-5, however, the outer tabernacle refers to the Holy Place and the inner tabernacle to the Most Holy Place. Various things related to the Old Testament priestly system are mentioned in these verses— the lampstand, the table and bread, the veil separating the Holy Place and the Most Holy Place, the altar of incense and the ark of the covenant which held the manna, Aaron's rod, and the Decalogue (see Leviticus 24 for more details concerning these things). Above the ark were the cherubim that guarded the mercy seat. After mentioning these things, the author says his purpose is not to speak in detail of things that were part of the former covenant.

9:6-10. The things mentioned in vv. 1-5 were used by the priests in their service. These matters are explained in detail in the Old Testament (see Exodus 25-40; Leviticus 24). The priests continually entered the Holy Place, described in this context as the outer tabernacle, to perform their tasks. But only the high priest entered into the inner tabernacle, the second place, the Most Holy Place. He entered once a year, on the Day of Atonement (Leviticus 16), always carrying the blood of a sacrifice which he offered first for himself and his own sins, and afterward for the sins of the people. It is specifically mentioned that this sacrifice was for sins committed unknowingly or in ignorance, a point that will become very important in the argument of the author in 10:26-31.

That these sacrifices were necessary continually, that the high priest had to enter the Most Holy Place annually, the author says is the Holy Spirit's way of showing that the method of entry into the Most Holy Place (the meaning of "holy place" in this verse) had not been revealed. Access to the very presence of God was limited as long as the outer tabernacle was standing and in use. The author is setting forth the preliminary and temporary nature of the previous covenant and the superiority of the new covenant. The lesson is for the present. Gifts and sacrifices that could not completely cleanse the conscience of the worshiper were offered continually. Under the first covenant, these sacrifices related to food, drink, washings, and physical regulations. These were temporary, to last only until a time of reformation. Reformation is literally "setting things right." This phrase refers to the new covenant established with the high priesthood of Jesus.

9:11-14. This section explains various aspects of the heavenly sanctuary, comparing the work of Christ to the system just described in 9:1-10, thus showing the superiority of Christ's sacrificial work.

"When Christ appeared...." The first phrase of v. 11 raises the question, "When did this occur?" Since the sacrifice was "once for all" it seems best to understand the verse as a reference to Jesus' sacrifice of himself on the cross after which he was prepared to serve as high priest. The context of 9:24-25 could seem to put this after the ascension, perhaps pointing to his entry to the presence of God as intercessor based on his perfect sacrifice. The point of the verse is not the exact timing. Christ as high priest brings better things.

As high priest Jesus entered the heavenly tabernacle, not with the blood of goats and calves but with his own blood as the sacrifice. He entered not for himself, but for the eternal redemption of all mankind (to obtain redemption, the aorist participle indicates a completed act). This heavenly sanctuary is called "the holy place" but corresponds to the "most holy place" in the earthly tabernacle, that is, to the very presence of God. This he did "once for all" (see 7:27; 9:28; 10:10). Thus, there is no need for a continuing repetition of this work.

9:13-14. The first class condition indicates that the statement is true: the blood of goats and bulls sprinkled on those who were unclean sanctified for cleansing the flesh because God accepted these sacrifices. "How much more" begins a comparison of the two covenants (compare 2:1-3; 3:3; 8:6; 10:28-29). How much more will the blood of Christ, offering himself without blemish through the eternal spirit, cleanse the human conscience from dead works to serve (*latreuo*, to serve in the sense of worship) the living God? This word is also used of Jesus' service as high priest (8:2). "Eternal spirit" is usually understood as Holy Spirit. "Dead works" is the same phrase as 6:1.

A summary comparing what is being said about the first system and the second system (referred to as different ministries, tabernacles, and covenants) helps one see the various contrasts.

The First Ministry	The Second Ministry
Earthly service—of this world	Heavenly service—not of this creation
Tabernacle made by humans	True tabernacle, not made with hands, built by God
High priests offering continuous sacrifices	Priesthood of Jesus, offering once for all forever
Way to Holy Place not open	Christ opens the way to access to God
Could not cleanse conscience	Cleanses conscience from dead works
Temporary—until time of reformation	Permanent—eternal promises

---

9:15-22. "Mediator" is repeated from 8:6 and relates to the new covenant. After showing that Jesus has a better ministry as high priest in Chapters 5-7, the author shows the superiority of the new covenant in Chapters 8-9, summarized in 10:1-18. The idea of a new covenant (Jer. 31:31-34; see also 7:22; 8:8-13; 10:15-17) would have been difficult for the Jews to accept. Thus, the author returns to this point. The argument of v. 15 uses the meaning of "covenant" as both "legal contract" and as "last will and testament."

9:15-17. Jesus' death was effective for the redemption of sins committed under the first covenant (see 9:12, redemption). This statement is necessarily true because those under the first covenant were also recipients of the promise of eternal inheritance. The Mosaic covenant served to demonstrate the incapacity of human creation to obey God's commands. None could fulfill the requirements of the Old Law. With the death of

Jesus, the new covenant became effective, reaching both backward and forward.

9:18-22. The first covenant depended on blood, as shown in Moses' actions to cleanse the people. The items used in the tabernacle (9:1-5) were cleansed with blood. According to the prior covenant, the Old Testament law, all things were cleansed with blood so that one could even say that forgiveness is impossible without blood being shed. In 9:20 is a citation from Ex. 24:8.

9:23-28. The Old Testament system was a copy of the celestial. In the same way that the earthly things were cleansed by sprinkling with blood (v. 22), so also it was necessary that the heavenly model be cleansed with better sacrifices. Why the heavenly things need to be cleansed is not fully explained. Perhaps it is the entry of sin into the human experience, perhaps the influence and presence of Satan, perhaps it is simply a concept that was known in rabbinical teachings. This cleansing was done through the high priesthood of Jesus. Christ did not enter the earthly holy place (Most Holy Place) made by hands, which is only a copy of the true Most Holy Place. Christ entered heaven itself to appear in God's presence. This reference to Christ's priestly work involves his sacrifice on earth and his presence before God in heaven as high priest. He appears (v. 24), he is manifest (v. 26), he will be seen (v. 28). The use of these three generally synonymous verbs may be due to the fact that each use refers to a different setting: he now appears in heaven, he was manifested on the earth, he will be seen in his coming.

The emphasis of the book of Hebrews is that Jesus' "once for all" offering replaces the annual offering of the high priest in the Levitical system. If Jesus had been a high priest under the previous covenant, he would have had to suffer often, again and again, beginning in the very foundation of the world when sin entered the human experience. But now, Jesus has sacrificed himself "once for all" to put away sin in the fulfillment or end of the ages. The focus is on the once and always sacrifice of Jesus, making his priesthood, ministry, sacrifice, sanctuary, and covenant superior.

9:27-28. Verse 27 is often quoted out of context. The point is that death followed by judgment is a sure part of the human experience. The reality cannot be denied. That men die once is used in this context to demonstrate the necessity of the "once for all" sacrifice of Jesus. Christ, having been offered once to bear sins, will one day come again (appear, be seen) a second time. This appearance will be to bring salvation, will not be for the purpose of dealing with sin, and will be welcomed by those who look for him expectantly. This statement refers to the Second Coming. Thinking about the two comings of Jesus—the Incarnation and his coming at the end of time, this verse says that Jesus came the first time to deal with the sin problem and will come again to gather those who are his. "To bear the sins of many" is a frequent concept in the New Testament, but here it may call to mind for the recipients the text of Isaiah 53:1-12.

Hebrews 10

[Note: it is suggested that the student read the introductory materials in this guide before beginning individual preparatory reading and analysis.]

CONTENT
The paragraphing included in the Content section provides suggestions or guides. The student is encouraged to identify the paragraphs to assist in his or her personal study. In this chapter, he division of this chapter into paragraphs is fairly standard in modern translations.

Outline of Chapter

10:1-10, Christ's sacrifice takes away sin, whereas the old sacrificial system was ineffective

10:11-18, Christ's death is effective to establish the new covenant with all of its benefits

10:19-25, exhortation and warning to come near to God to receive the promises

10:26-31, the danger of apostasy, willful or intentional sin

10:32-39, reasons for perseverance—receiving the promise

Overview of Chapter

The literary unit that began in 8:1 concludes in 10:18. The extended section concerning Jesus' high priesthood (5:1-10:18) also concludes. The first part of this chapter (vv. 1-18) summarizes the ways in which Jesus' priesthood is superior to the ministry of the Levitical priests: he offered his own blood, it was "once for all," it opened the way to the heavenly sanctuary. The focus on perfection, maturity, completeness (*teleioo*) continues (2:10; 5:9; 7:19, 28; 9:9; 10:1; 11:40; 12:23).

The final teaching section of Hebrews (10:19-12:29) sets forth the better promises that Jesus brings under the new covenant. The fourth admonition (10:22) is based on what has come before—it is time to draw near to God through Jesus' ministry and the new covenant, because only in drawing near can one receive that which has been promised.

Purposefully turning away from God was punishable by death under the first covenant. How much more severe will be the punishment for those who turn their back on the final, unchangeable sacrifice of Jesus? It is time to persevere; it is not time to draw back because the one who draws back can never please God.

STUDY HELPS
10:1-10. Much of the first part of this chapter is summary. The law was only a shadow; it was not the reality of the things that were to come. The contrast is explained in various ways in the book of Hebrews. In 8:5, the celestial is a model (*tupos*); the earthly was only an example (*hupodeigmati*, representation, figure, or copy) and a shadow (*skia*).

In 10:1, the law is a shadow (*skia*), but the comparison is used in a different way. The law foreshadowed the good things to come (cf. 9:11). It was not the true form of the realities (*eikon*, image). It corresponded to the real thing as a reproduction corresponds to the real thing, but it was only a shadow. The law with its ordinances could not cleanse the consciences of those who drew near. This fact is obvious because the same sacrifices were offered continually. If genuine cleansing had been possible, the offerings would have ceased, because once a worshiper is really cleansed there is no more consciousness of sins (v. 2). This lack of perpetual cleansing was the problem with the Levitical system. The annual sacrifices were a reminder of the presence of sins and of the fact that the sacrifices did not make perfect (*teleioo*) those who drew near. Remember that *telos* is also the term for maturity and is used in connection with the priesthood of Melchizedek (7:11) and the heavenly tabernacle (9:11). Those who drew near in the Old Testament were the priests, but the reference here corresponds to all believers in the new covenant who approach God in worship and have access to God (4:16; 7:19, 25; 10:1, 22).

The continual repetition of sacrifices was necessary under the previous covenant because the blood of animals did not take away sins—such was impossible. (For the use of impossible in the book, see 6:4, 6, 18; 10:4; 11:6). In vv. 5-7 this claim is supported with a quotation from Ps. 40:6-8. Verses 8-10 explain the application the author is making of this Old Testament passage.

God's ultimate desire was not in the sacrifices and offerings of the Old Testament system, although he accepted these for a time. God had a plan that extended beyond the nation of Israel. The passage from the Psalms is applied to Jesus as one who comes to do God's will, that is, to establish a new covenant that would open to all humanity access to God. Jesus came to do God's will and he did it voluntarily. In v. 8, the use of various words to describe the Old Testament sacrificial system applies to the different types of offerings described in the Old Testament, offered according to the law. All of these pointed forward to the sacrificial work of Christ.

10:9. The antecedent of the pronoun is not clear, referring either to the Father or to Jesus. The point is not important to the interpretation of the text which clearly shows the inauguration of a new covenant. He "does away" with the first. The verb means "to destroy." This description must be understood in the context of other New Testament passages that describe the covenant as "fulfilled" or "abolished." In replacing the first, he opens the way for the second, the covenant established on the basis of Jesus' high priesthood (Jer. 31:31-34). Remember the statement in 7:11-12 that the replacement of the previous high priestly system requires also the replacement of the covenant that corresponded to it. The new covenant replaces the former covenant.

10:10. It is God's will that we be sanctified through the sacrifice of Jesus "once for all." The question can be raised, does this refer to God's will or Christ's will? The focus is on sanctification as God's will (1 Th. 4:8). This sanctification is accomplished through the body of Jesus. The phrase "once for all" is often repeated in Hebrews (7:27; 9:12, 28; 10:10) and is a primary point in demonstrating the superiority of Jesus' sacrifice.

10:11-18. In Hebrews, Jesus is described as both priest and high priest. Some manuscripts read high priest in v. 11. The point is that the priests under the Levitical sacrificial system offered the same sacrifices again and again. Some of these were daily sacrifices, but the sacrifice offered by the high priest was offered annually on the Day of Atonement. The continual offering of such sacrifices demonstrates that sins were not removed by such sacrifices. In this final paragraph of the extended section, we have the summary of 8:1-10:18. Jesus made one sacrifice forever, and was thus able to enter the presence of God (the celestial Most Holy Place) permanently to sit down at God's right hand (as described in 9:24ff; also see Psalm 110). Jesus' sacrifice permanently solves the sin problem of humanity.

10:13-18. The reference to Ps. 110:1 indicates that Jesus has won the victory over his enemies, even though the final verdict has not yet been rendered. The perfection of those who are sanctified is certain, as was predicted in Jer. 31:31-34. That believers must continue in faithful response has been made clear throughout the book of Hebrews. There is no question about the adequacy of Jesus' ministry; the question is about faithful response on the part of human beings. Note that the Old Testament citation is attributed to the Holy Spirit.

The quotation from Jer. 31:31-34 serves to solidify the author's point. It ties together the section (8:1-10:18), repeating the quotation that was used in 8:7-13. The order of the phrases in the citation is reversed—perhaps the author is writing from memory. These verses describe the result accomplished with the coming of the new covenant. Verse 18 contains a brief summary of the argument: where there is genuine forgiveness, sin offerings are no longer necessary.

The Development of the Message of Hebrews

4:14-7:28	A Better Ministry
8:1-6	"This is the point...."
8:6	Better ministry, covenant, promises
8:7-10:18	A Better Covenant
10:19-12:29	Better Promises
10:22-25	Fourth Exhortation: Draw Near
12:14-16	Fifth Exhortation: Be Careful
Chapter 13	Final Imperatives

10:19-25. This section includes the fourth warning or exhortation of the book, and moves the argument of the writer to the next step. Based on the high priesthood of Jesus, we have confidence (boldness) to enter the holy place (referring to the celestial Most Holy Place) by Jesus' blood. With his sacrifice, he opened a new and living way through the curtain (between the Holy Place and the Most Holy Place). The text may seem to identify the flesh of Jesus with the curtain, but a better reading is that "he opened a way through the curtain, that is, he opened a way through his flesh," meaning through his death. The reading does not use repetition to identity Jesus' flesh with the curtain; the verse contains two affirmations.

Fourth Exhortation

...let us approach with a true heart in full confidence of faith, our hearts sprinkled from an evil conscience and our bodies washed with pure water. Let us hold on firmly to the confession of our hope, because faithful is the one who promised. And let us consider how to motivate one another to love and good works, not leaving behind our gathering together. --Hebrews 10:22-25a

---

The confidence we have is held fast by faith. We have continual access to God because the veil of separation has been removed through Jesus' death. This veil was torn apart on the day of the crucifixion (Matt. 27:51). That Jesus opened (the aorist active verb indicates an accomplished action) a new and living way may refer to the dead works mentioned previously in the book or to the slain sacrifices. In comparison, Jesus is alive. Our access to God is possible because we have a great high priest.

That we have a great high priest gives us confidence to draw near. The redemptive work of Christ must be accepted and applied. Through Christ we approach God. This section has three imperatives: let us draw near, let us hold fast, let us consider (vv. 22-24). The first of these imperatives, "drawing near," requires a sincere heart, assurance of faith, a clean (sprinkled) heart, and a washed body. Sincerity relates to attitude. In the book of Hebrews, full assurance is tied to faith. Assurance must be accepted as a clear biblical teaching; it is to be demonstrated by one's life. Assurance is the result of faith. Christians do not live apathetic, faithless, unfruitful, godless, worldly lives. Sprinkling in this context likely relates to the sprinkling of blood that was part of the first covenant, which is used to describe Christ's sacrifice (9:9, 14). This sprinkling applied in the context of the new covenant cleanses consciences, something that was not possible with the sprinkling of the blood of animals in the Old Testament (9:9; 10:2).

In this context, washing may be designed to remind of the actions of the high priest. Here it is applied to Christians as a requirement for drawing near to God with a clean conscience. Of interest is that 1 Pet. 3:21 also makes a connection between baptism and a clean conscience. Despite the desire of many to deny any application to baptism in the context of Hebrews, one must consider the possibility that the reference to bodies washed with pure water, while based on the actions of the Old Testament priesthood, is applied here in parallel to the actions of the high priest under the new covenant, a washing that occurs figuratively in baptism when the human conscience answers God and is cleansed. The New Testament clearly speaks of baptism as a washing away of sin (Acts 22:16; 1 Cor. 6;11; Eph. 5:26; Titus 3:5; 1 Pet. 3:21).

The second imperative, "let us hold fast," is based on the promise of God and God's faithfulness (6:13-20). The imperatives describe the actions expected of a believer who has access to God on the basis of the new covenant. In this section of the book begins a focus on the better promises of God (see 8:6). We confess hope. Responsive faith believes God and therefore does not waver (Rom. 4:17-21; Heb. 11:11). The one who has promised is faithful. Note the increasing emphasis on the promises of God.

The third imperative, "let us consider one another," is followed by a series of participles that explain how we are to consider one another: stimulating one another to love and good deeds, not forsaking the assemblies, and encouraging one another. "Stimulate" is a strong verb that is often negative. Here the results are positive, but the stimulation may not be enjoyable. "Assembling together" comes from the root word that also gives us the word synagogue. In this verse is the only use of this verb in the New Testament. The passage should not be used to teach that these Christians were assembling for worship in synagogues. The admonition "to encourage" one another is tied to the approaching "day." Some have seen in this phrase a reference to the destruction of Jerusalem; others note that in the context of the verses that follow, a reference to the Second Coming and the Day of Judgment seems more natural (also compare 9:27-28). One's interpretation of "the day" will obviously influence the date assigned to the book. The point of the teaching is that Christians are expected to gather and to encourage one another.

10:26-31. The tendency of Western thought is to try to establish a clear outline based on divisions in the text. The Eastern method of thought development is different. The passage in 10:19-25 is clearly exhortatory. In this paragraph (10:26-31), the exhortation and warning continue. The previous section encouraged positive actions: draw near, hold fast, consider and encourage. This section describes what will happen to those who reject truth in disbelief and disobedience. This passage clearly relates to the warning of 3:7-19.

Consider this summary of vv. 26-31. "The last sacrifice for sin has been made. Therefore, if we go on sinning willfully (intentionally) after knowing the truth, there is not another sin sacrifice (v. 26). All that remains are judgment and consuming fire that will be unleashed on the adversaries (v. 27). The writer is not presenting a new principle or teaching. Even under the Law of Moses, if one rejected the law, that one died with no mercy extended, on the basis of witness testimony (v. 28). If the law of Moses functioned in this way, how much more severe is the punishment deserved when one tramples the very Son of God (not merely a servant in the house, Moses), and considers as unclean the blood of Jesus, the blood of the new and final covenant, the blood that sanctifies? How much more severe will be the punishment for one who insults the Spirit of grace (v. 29)? God himself in the Old Testament claimed vengeance, retribution, and judgment as his (v. 30). To fall into the hands of this God without remedy is indeed fearful (v. 31)."

It may be surprising that the author uses "we." This use is likely a literary technique and does mean that the author is among those who have demonstrated such an attitude. The subject is willful sin. Willful sin existed under the Old Testament and was severely punished (Num. 15:22-31). No sacrifice existed to cover willful sin. The sacrifice of the high priest was for unintentional sin (see Heb. 5:2). Intentional sin is described in the Old Testament as a sin "of the high hand." In the biblical text in Hebrews, the sin being considered is the intentional rejection of Jesus. Such rejection is especially dangerous because it occurs after receiving the truth (cf. 6:4-6). Rejecting Jesus without knowledge is one thing; rejecting Jesus after having knowledge is another and makes renewal or restoration difficult if not impossible.

We must make certain that our own biases and previous misunderstandings do not color our understanding and application of this text. In 10:26-31, the issue is not sin in the lives of believers. The issue is unbelief among those who previously believed. The passage is about those who totally turn their back on Jesus. Without doubt, it is possible to leave the path after beginning the journey, but let us be careful in drawing contemporary lessons based on these verses. Repeated sin in the life of a Christian today may indicate unbelief, but it may indicate weakness and the need for spiritual growth.

10:27-29. While the book of Hebrews focuses on hope, the negative aspect of anticipation is also a possibility—judgment is coming. Judgment was a part of the Old Testament system as evidenced by the death of those who willfully set aside (rejected, violated, disobeyed) the law. How much more severe will be the punishment under the new covenant? This comparison presents an argument from the lesser to the greater. "To trample underfoot" means to treat with contempt. The reference to the "Son of God" continues the argument of the book that Jesus is better because he is a Son. "Regarded" implies making a choice. It is beyond imagination that one would reject sanctification after receiving it. That sanctification has been received implies a rejection after the fact, that is, not an initial rejection of the covenant but a turning away from the covenant after receiving the benefits of Jesus' high priesthood. "Insulting the Spirit of grace" likely refers to the Holy Spirit as the one revealing the gracious offer of the new covenant.

10:30-31. Quotations from Deut. 32:35-36 are used to show that God, under the first covenant, was a God of vengeance, retribution (repayment), and judgment. God's nature has not changed. To contemplate the consequences of unbelief is a fearful thing.

10:32-39. We have previously noted that the section that begins in 10:19 calls attention to God's better promises (8:6) that are available under the better covenant. The importance of this truth is made clearer by the teachings in the last part of Chapter 10. The recipients of the book had formerly been enlightened. Since the group in 6:4 had also been enlightened but had reached a point where they could not be restored, and since the author is trying through admonition and warning to influence the recipients toward restored faith, it seems that 6:4 does not describe the same group as 10:32 (see comments at 6:4-6). The recipients had endured conflict and suffering, had been made spectacles through reproach and tribulation, and had shared with those who were mistreated (vv. 32-33). They had helped others, thus sharing in the reproach. They had had property plundered, but they accepted such loss with the assurance of a better and eternal possession.

To understand this section, contrast the description in vv. 26-31 with the "you" of vv. 32-39. (Remember the same contrast in 6:4-8 and 6:9-12). Some had rejected the message of Christ. On the other hand, the recipients had begun well but were apparently having doubts. Thus, the author admonishes them not to throw away their confidence (3:6; 4:16; 10:19) but rather with the same faith in the One who promises (Chapter 11) to endure (12:1-3). Genuine faith perseveres. The question is, what will we do when difficulties come? God is faithful; his promises are secure. The reward is certain. The great need of the church is faithful endurance so as to receive what has been promised. Maintain confidence. Confidence is rewarded. The way to receive the better promises of the new covenant is to persevere.

The author uses an Old Testament citation to cement his point. In 10:37-38 is found a quotation from Hab. 2:3-4. The

LXX varies from the Hebrew text; the author makes his point based on the reading in the LXX. The Habakkuk passage is well-known to most Bible students, but the application of the author of Hebrews may catch us off guard since the LXX reading is less well-known. "If anyone shrinks back, my soul has no pleasure in him." The Messiah is coming, the just live by faith, those who shrink from faith cannot be pleasing to God.

The author concludes the chapter with firm assurance concerning the perseverance of his readers (cf. 6:9-12 for the same confidence of response). We will not shrink back to destruction; we will persevere in faith and preserve (save) our souls. A great danger in Christianity is shrinking back.

Hebrews 11

[Note: it is suggested that the student read the introductory materials in this guide before beginning individual preparatory reading and analysis.]

CONTENT
The paragraphing in the Content section of each chapter is only a suggestion. Paragraphs can be identified in this chapter, but the comments below are organized consecutively by person or topic. The student is always encouraged to identify the paragraphs.

In this chapter, dividing the text according to the persons mentioned, while noticing the summary verses, seems easier. The specific examples given by the author are followed by a summary of the chapter in vv. 39-40.

Outline of Chapter
11:1-38, "by faith...."
    1, faith defined—two aspects of faith are conviction and confidence
    2, by faith our forefathers gave good testimony
    3, in the creation
    4, Abel
    5, Enoch
      6, summary
    7, Noah
    8, Abraham
    11, Sarah
      13-16, summary
    17, Abraham
    20-22, Isaac, Jacob and Joseph
    23, Moses
    30-31, Jericho and Rahab
      32-38, many more
11:39-40, by faith they overcame

Overview of Chapter

Chapter 11 contains a series of Old Testament mini-stories of those who were faithful in difficult circumstances. These serve as examples. The descriptions of these Old Testament personages repeat many of the key phrases in the book. These are examples of those who did not shrink back (10:37-39).

The point is that one must be faithful (believing and obedient) in every circumstance, just as were these heroes of faith. In the lives of these people, one sees faith lived out, not just faith confessed with the mouth.

Note the emphasis on the promises of God in this chapter. While Hebrews 11 is often labeled the "Faith Chapter," one can also note that the large number of references to the promise (including concepts such as future, inheritance, and hope). By my count, there are 21 direct or indirect references to the promise in this section (10:19-11:40).

STUDY HELPS
11:1-2. Faith is necessary to receive the promises of God. Faith is based on confidence in the promise, and in the one making the promise. This makes the promise primary.

Verse 1 is not a definition of faith but a description. Faith is confidence and conviction. Faith "stands under" and thus provides foundation, confidence and assurance. The same word is used in 1:3 and 3:14. Faith is the opposite of apostasy or falling away. The word translated "conviction" appears only here in the New Testament. It means "to prove by testing." Those mentioned in this chapter did not see what was promised, but they had confidence in God and in God's promises. They were approved on the basis of their faithful response. They did not see the fulfillment of the promise; they believed things that were for them unseen. They were hopeful because they counted as faithful the one making the promise. These two concepts run as threads throughout the chapter. Two aspects or dimensions of faith are described in these verses: faith is conviction regarding things that are not seen, faith is confidence in God's promises and assurance of things hoped for.

Faith is human response to God's faithfulness. In Romans 3, the Bible speaks of the faith of Christ. In the context of

Romans, the reference to "the faith of Christ" is not to our faith in Christ but to Christ's faithfulness, that is, Christ's faithful response to God.

11:3. By faith the creation of the universe is understood, that God prepared the world by his word (*rhema*) and created something out of nothing, things visible from things invisible. This last phrase points to an important dimension of faith—faith in what is not seen or personally experienced, faith based solely in the revelation and promise of God.

11:4. Abel offered a better sacrifice (notice the continuing theme of better), which gave testimony that he was righteous. This he did by faith in what was for him yet unseen. His example speaks to us even though he is now dead, killed by his brother.

11:5. Enoch (Gen. 5:24) did not die. The Bible does not give details but simply says that he walked with God. He was taken up, meaning that he was "translated" just as was Elijah (2 Kings 2:11). He acted by faith and his life bears testimony that he was pleasing to God. He believed in that which is not seen.

11:6. Verse 6 is a key verse in understanding the chapter. Faith not only begins—faith perseveres. The examples of faith that are included in this chapter are persons who remained faithful because they were looking beyond this life to the reward, to the things promised. They believed in what was for them unseen, and they believed that God is faithful to reward those who seek him. Faith is essential to pleasing God. This faith includes belief in God's existence, and faith that God will fulfill his promises in the future. Neither aspect of faith is optional. This verse reflects the same two dimensions of faith that were introduced in v. 1.

11:7. Noah was warned about things that he had never seen or experienced previously, and by faith he built an ark to save his household. He acted in hope. Noah's faithful action served to condemn the world and made him an heir of the righteousness; this was the result of his faith. Here is the pattern: faith acts on what God provides. Faith operates in the realm of the invisible and the unseen. Faith operates on the basis of hope.

11:8-10. Abraham also acted by faith. Abraham's faith is first seen in that he obeyed when he was called. He left his own country, not knowing where he was going, and went out to receive an inheritance that God had promised. He lived as a foreigner in the land of promise, in temporary housing with his son and grandson who also shared the promise. Here the author notes that the Promised Land to which Moses and the Israelites journeyed was also the "land of promise" to Abraham. Abraham obeyed because he was seeing the unseen, looking continually for a city built by God.

11:11-12. Sarah, beyond the normal age span of fertility, received the ability to conceive because she considered God faithful in his promise. Here Sarah's faith is based on God's faithfulness and looks to God's promise. In contrast, the story in Genesis says that Sarah tried to help God by giving Abraham her maidservant and that she laughed at the promise. Even so, the result was the fulfillment of God's promise.

11:13-16. In a brief summary, the author notes that all of these died in faith (having acted by faith) without receiving the promises. They died without having seen, yet they maintained hope. This hope is the essence of faith. The author draws a comparison between the recipients of the book and the Old Testament patriarchs. The patriarchs, although they could see only from a distance, did not shrink back but joyfully lived in anticipation of receiving their inheritance. Had they been of those who shrink back, they had ample opportunities to turn back. They desired something better, something the author describes as heavenly (cf. heavenly calling in 3:1; heavenly gift in 6:4, the contrast between the earthly and the heavenly in Chapters 8-9). Faith is a spiritual reality that has an impact in the physical realm. Therefore, God is not ashamed to be called their God (2:11; 8:10). God is faithful and fulfills his promises.

11:17-19. Returning to Abraham, the author notes that Abraham offered Isaac when he was tested, again on the basis of the promise he had received from God. Abraham's faithful response was based on God's promise. The use of "only begotten" (*monogenes*) in this context is helpful to our understanding of the use of the word in first century Koine Greek. Since Abraham had other children, it cannot mean that Isaac was the only son Abraham bore, but rather refers to the "only being" (unique) son of Abraham, that is, the son of promise. This word appears in John 3:16 with reference to Jesus. In 11:18, God made the promise to Abraham before he tested him (Genesis 22). Abraham believed in God's power to resurrect from the dead, and in a figure or type his faith foreshadows God's resurrection power in Jesus.

11:20-22. Isaac blessed his sons. Jacob blessed the sons of Joseph. Joseph mentioned the exodus from Egypt when he gave orders concerning his bones. These three cases all point to examples of faith in God's ability to fulfill promises.

11:23-29. Moses is next mentioned as one who acted by faith. The Moses story is summarized—his birth, being hidden by his parents, being raised by Pharaoh's daughter, and then as an adult rejecting those privileges to lead God's people. Moses kept his eye on the future and God's promises, not on his current situation. He chose suffering rather than sin, he chose reproach rather than riches, he chose the eternal reward rather than the present ease. The idea of looking forward to a reward points again to God's promises. The idea of not fearing the king appears twice in the passage suggesting the need to look beyond present threats and dangers. Moses endured, seeing the God who is unseen. He kept the Passover, the sprinkling of blood, and thus escaped the wrath of God that came on the firstborn. As he led the people out of Egypt, they passed through the Red Sea while the Egyptians attempting to do the same were drowned. Here are multiple references to God's instructions and God's promises which Moses faithfully kept and honored.

11:30-31. The account of the fall of Jericho and the saving of Rahab give examples of what it means to act by faith. The

Israelites obeyed a command that perhaps seemed foolish, and the walls fell. Rahab by faith did not perish with the disobedient. Her faith and obedience are also mentioned in James 2:25.

11:32-38. The author continues by noting that time will not permit the mention of many others who acted by faith—Gideon, Barak, Samson, Jephthah, David, Samuel and the prophets. He describes their faithful actions in this way:

> "...they conquered kingdoms, acted righteously, obtained promises, shut the mouths of lions, quenched the power of fire, escaped the sword, were strong in weakness, mighty in war, and put foreign armies to flight. Women received back their dead by resurrection; some were tortured and would not agree to unfaithful actions in order to secure their release. They hoped for a better resurrection. Some experienced mocking, scourging, chains and imprisonment. Some were stoned, sawn in two, tempted, and killed with the sword. They were destitute without the basic necessities of this world."

This history reflects the persecution that many of God's people suffered. Some of these things are described in more detail in the Old Testament.

It is not hard to see and understand the message that is communicated in this summary. Are we to be surprised when the Christian life is not easy? Should we not expect difficulties as well as they?

11:39-40. These who have been mentioned were approved by their faith, even though they did not receive what was promised. An inclusion is formed by 11:2 and 11:39—they were commended. They received a testimony. They are witnesses with a testimony. Their testimony is that God is faithful and that God's promises are certain. They lived without seeing the end; they lived in hope. God was working through them to provide for us better things through better promises. God's promises were delayed so that these Old Testament examples did not reach perfection (maturity, completeness) apart from the faithful followers of future generations. Note the continuing emphasis on better, perfection, and promises.

Hebrews 12

[Note: it is suggested that the student read the introductory materials in this guide before beginning individual preparatory reading and analysis.]

CONTENT
The paragraphing included in the Content section of each chapter provides suggestions or guides. The student is encouraged to read the text, analyze the thought patterns, and identify the paragraphs and the subsections within each paragraph, to assist in his or her personal study. The division of the text into paragraphs is fairly standard in modern translations.

Outline of Chapter
12:1-2, the example of Jesus Christ
12:3-11, God disciplines us as a Father does his children
12:12-17, warning against rejecting God's grace
12:18-29, final comparison of the two covenants and the promised blessings of God

Overview of Chapter
 This chapter finalizes the extended argument of the author of Hebrews concerning the ministry, covenant, and promises of Jesus as High Priest, in comparison to the ministry, covenant and promises of the previous priestly system.
 The fifth and final warning and exhortation is found in the paragraph of 12:12-17.
 The author's treatment of God's better promises is brought to a climax as the section (10:19-12:29) concludes.

STUDY HELPS
12:1-2. These two verses are perhaps not deserving of treatment as a separate paragraph, but the construction of the sentences in Greek complicates the division of the chapter. These two verses provide a bridge from Chapter 11 and an introduction to Chapter 12.

Those mentioned in Chapter 11 are described as witnesses. This may mean that they give testimony to God's faithfulness and the certainty of God's promises, that they can testify to the value of following faithfully and obediently. The word sometimes refers to a martyr. It can also be used to refer to observers. The first two options best fit the context. The author is saying something more than that we are surrounded by observers. "They" received a good testimony (11:39-40). In view of the faithfulness of these witnesses who have run the race before us, let us run faithfully. They are our examples; let us follow their example.

Four things are mentioned about how we should run the race: laying aside every encumbrance, laying aside sin, with endurance, keeping eyes fixed on Jesus. Laying aside encumbrances is like taking off a garment or removing weights. Sin is described as entangling us or tripping us. Jesus as our merciful and faithful high priest can help us with the things that weigh us down (he is merciful) and with our sin (he is faithful).

The goal is to run and finish the race. This requires endurance. Endurance is an important concept in the book of Hebrews. In some translations, it is called perseverance. Finally, we are to fix our eyes on Jesus. This means to look intently, to analyze and watch carefully. Jesus is described as the author (cf. 2:10, pioneer) and perfecter (finisher, *teleiotes*) of faith. He is beginning and end.

Jesus, for the joy set before him endured the cross, despised the shame, and is now seated at God's right hand. His endurance led to his exaltation. "Set before him" reminds of the race set before us. The challenge is to fulfill God's will in our lives. Here is a brief summary of the high priestly work of Jesus through which he made sacrifice, identified with God's people, and now intercedes.

12:3-11. Consider Jesus. The verb means "to add it up." Think of all that has been said about Jesus and arrive at a conclusion. Jesus endured shameful treatment and was killed, shedding his blood on the cross. When one considers what Jesus endured, one is encouraged not to "grow weary" and "lose heart". These two verbs are athletic terms that describe breathing very hard and collapsing after a race. Jesus endured much more than the recipients have endured. "You have not resisted to the point of shedding blood." Christians struggle against sin. Jesus' struggle against sin was much more intense.

The quotation from Prov. 3:11-12 is introduced with a question that suggests that part of the problem for the Hebrews was that they were not remembering some basic teachings of the Old Testament. The discipline of the Lord, such as a father uses to train a child, is to be expected for those who are genuinely children. Just as earthly parents discipline their children, so the Lord disciplines his children. This discipline is an evidence of his love. To the extent that the things being endured are used by God to teach us, to that same extent we can be sure of God's love for us as sons. Jesus is a son; we are sons. If we are not disciplined by God, how can we truly claim to be sons (v. 8)? If earthly fathers are respected because they love and discipline their children, how much more should we love, respect, and be subject to the heavenly Father (Father of spirits, probably referring to God as the source of all life)?

12:10-11. Because we are children, God disciplines us for our good. One result is that we share his holiness (cf. 2:9-10, 11-13). God's discipline is a part of our sanctification and leads us to righteousness. Discipline is not enjoyable, but those who receive it are blessed.

Fifth Exhortation
Pursue peace with everyone, and holiness, without which no one will see the Lord. Watch diligently lest any fall short of the grace of God...and that no one be an immoral and profane person like Esau.... --Hebrews 12:14, 15a, 16a

---

12:12-17. In this passage is the fifth and final exhortation in the book of Hebrews. There is an allusion to Isa. 35:3, a text that may provide background for the entire chapter. "Strengthen" is more literally to "make straight" and connects to the next verse. Verse 13 may be an allusion to Prov. 4:26. The goal is strength where there was weakness, healing where there was incapacity. The application is made in vv. 14-17.

"Pursue peace" is an imperative and is linked here with sanctification or holiness (v. 10, cf. 2:11). It is also connected with discipline. The author says that without sanctification no one will see the Lord. "See the Lord" may recall the need to fix our eyes on Jesus. "See to it" functions also as an imperative, since it is a dependent participle related to the preceding imperative. Here is the heart of the admonition: it is possible to come short of God's grace, to fail to attain it. Do not miss God's grace. It is possible to become embittered when problems come. Bitterness is described as a cause of trouble in v. 15. Such attitudes and responses defile a person. These are serious warnings in view of the possibility of shrinking back and rejecting Jesus.

Esau is set forth as an example of bitterness; Esau is an example of failing to attain. Perhaps this example is used in this context because Esau is one who received God's promises but did not act on them. He was rejected even though he later changed his mind. The application is clear: now is the time to make the decision. Esau could not recover his inheritance and was rejected even though he "tearfully sought it." He sold his birthright because he was hungry. He suffered a very small difficulty and made the wrong decision. The author is suggesting that the recipients may be in danger of doing the same thing.

12:18-29. This section serves as a conclusion to Chapters 5-12. One last time, the author describes and contrasts the Mosaic law and the new covenant. In 12:18-21 are various details about the giving of the Law on Mt. Sinai, with several Old Testament quotations. In contrast to the Sinai mountain of the Old Testament, those who live in the new covenant come to Mount Zion, heavenly Jerusalem, a new city. They come to an assembly of firstborn ones (the word is plural) who are enrolled in heaven. They come to God who is the Judge of all, and to genuine perfection (maturity, completeness), including the spirits of those righteous ones who lived under the old covenant (11:40) as well as those who live under the new covenant. They come to Jesus as mediator of the new covenant. They come to sprinkled blood that can cleanse the conscience (9:19; 10:22). Jesus' death had a much deeper meaning than the death of Abel. Abel's example is described as speaking or giving testimony after his death (11:4). Jesus' example speaks even more clearly as we look to him and draw near to God.

The conclusion: do not refuse this message (v. 25). One must respond. Some see in this verse another warning. It is similar to the first warning in 2:1-4. A decision is necessary. One must decide. When God gave the law at Sinai (v. 26), the earth shook. In Haggai 2:6 God promises to shake both heaven and earth, referring to the new and better temple. The author uses this comparison to note the necessity of listening to God as he warns from heaven.

The author's point is that some things are unshakeable, immovable, and set with certainty. Among these things is the kingdom established through the high priesthood of Jesus who is now both priest and king. The items related to the tabernacle and worship under the first covenant were temporal. The eternal kingdom is immovable. Let us be grateful. Let us worship God with reverence and awe. The consuming fire may refer to Mt. Sinai (Deut. 4:24), but also reminds of 10:31. Whatever we do, we must listen and faithfully obey when God speaks.

Hebrews 13

[Note: it is suggested that the student read the introductory materials in this guide before beginning individual preparatory reading and analysis.]

CONTENT
The paragraphing below is only a suggestion. The student is encouraged to identify paragraphs and subsections within the paragraphs to assist in personal study. The division of this chapter is difficult, especially in vv. 1-19.

Outline of Chapter
13:1-19, concluding instructions
13:20-21, blessing or benediction
13:22-25, concluding salutations

Overview of Chapter
    This last chapter makes the book look like a letter, even though the book does not begin with the traditional Greek letter form.
    Chapter 13 has several imperatives. Depending on how one counts the verbs and participial forms, there are at least 10 verb forms that can function as imperatives. Many of these imperatives exist in short sentences and are not expanded. Some sentences function as imperatives but do not have a verb.
    It may be helpful to define subsections in vv. 1-19, but I have chosen to treat these verses as one section in the outline above. The Study Helps are organized by smaller thought units.

STUDY HELPS
13:1. Let brotherly love (*philadelphia*) continue or abide (third person imperative).

13:2. Do not neglect (imperative) to show hospitality to strangers (literally, love to strangers). The verse perhaps refers to Genesis 18 when Abraham entertained three angels who appeared as humans. This verse does not teach that we are visited by angels today. The word angel means messenger and refers to other human beings in the context of showing love to strangers.

13:3. Remember (imperative) the prisoners (10:32-36). Some were imprisoned, not for doing evil, but because of their faith. Such was a common occurrence in the first century. Unfortunately, it is occurring today with increasing frequency. The reason for remembering others is that we are all part of one body, likely a reference to the church.

13:4. Marriage is to be honored (the imperative is understood, there is no verb in this sentence). The marriage bed is to be undefiled. Marriage is God's plan and was given to avoid fornication and adultery (1 Cor. 7:1-4). God provided for the sexual needs of human beings and will judge fornicators and adulterers.

13:5-6. Christians are to be content with what they have, being free from the love of money. There is no verb, although an imperative is implied. One reason Christians can be content is because God is ever present and always available to help. The quotation is from Psalms 118:6. There is no need to fear, whatever the circumstances. This reminds of Jesus the merciful high priest who understands our circumstances.

13:7. Remember (imperative) your leaders who spoke God's word to you. This refers to leaders in times past, those who first shared the gospel with them (cf. 2:1-4). The instruction is to consider (the dependent participle functions as an imperative because the verb on which it depends is an imperative) their conduct and imitate (imperative) their faith. The reference may be to those mentioned in Chapter 11. One task of Christian leaders is to speak the word of God. The word for leaders is a participial form from *hegeomai* (to govern or rule). The author uses a different word than would be expected if the reference were to the leadership group described in the New Testament as elders, bishops, or pastors.

13:8-9. Jesus is unchanging. Therefore, do not be carried away (imperative) by strange teachings. This instruction may relate to the temptation to shrink back (10:32-39). In the context, the strange teachings may have to do with ideas about which foods are acceptable and which are prohibited. The strange teachings may have to do with various Jewish practices. Real strength that firmly establishes our hearts comes through God's grace, not through laws about rituals, sacrifices, meals, and such like, which provide no benefit.

13:10-14. The altar mentioned here is the spiritual (heavenly) tabernacle. We have the benefit of Jesus' sacrificial work and those who served as priests under the first covenant do not automatically have the right to partake of this altar. In the Old Testament system (v. 11, see Lev. 16:27), the blood of animals was used in the (Most) Holy Place by the high priest as a sin offering and the body of the sacrificial animal was burned outside the camp. Jesus likewise, in order to sanctify his people with his blood, was crucified outside the gate, that is outside the city. The author's conclusion is that Christians must be willing to bear reproach with Christ. Doing this will involve going outside the camp (leaving the shelter of our comfort zones?). The argument is clear but the application is more difficult. Going outside the city may refer to seeking the lasting city that is to come, thus leaving the present city which would then be a metaphor for Judaism (v. 14).

13:15-16. Through Jesus we offer sacrificial praise, the fruit of our lips, giving thanks to his name. Doing good and sharing with others is also declared to be a type of sacrifice.

13:17. In this verse are two more imperatives: obey and submit. The word for leaders is the same Greek word as was used in v. 7. This verse must refer to the current leaders. There are two Greek words for obey. The word used here means "allow yourselves to be influenced by them." Instruction about submitting to leaders must be balanced by instruction to leaders against authoritarianism. These leaders keep watch and will give account. They are stewards. They have a specific ministry for which they are responsible. This verse is often used today to describe the responsibility of pastors to watch over or care for the church.

13:18-19. In a list of additional instructions reminiscent of the ending of many of the New Testament letters, the author urges prayer with several results in mind: a good conscience, honorable conduct, and that the author be able to visit them again. Every Christian could pray about such things with profit—for self, for others, and especially for those who lead.

13:20-21. These verses contain a benediction or doxology. The God of peace resurrected Jesus, who was made the Shepherd of the sheep through his sacrifice that established an eternal covenant (the new covenant). May this God equip you for every good thing to do his will, working that which is pleasing, to his glory.

13:22-25. The author refers to the book as a word of exhortation. Here is another imperative: "bear with this exhortation." The author knows Timothy. The reference to "Brother Timothy" is not consistent with Paul's customary way of using the term brother, a factor that is often seen as another evidence against the authorship of Paul. The mention of Timothy puts the date of the book during Timothy's lifetime. If Timothy visits the recipients, the author will see them as well. This perhaps implies that Timothy was a co-worker of the author, or that they sometimes worked together. The greetings to the leaders and saints (Christians) is customary letter form. The salutation referring to those from Italy is ambiguous. In the final phrase, "Grace be with you all," you is in the plural form.

The Message of Hebrews

[Note: This summary of the message of Hebrews has been adapted from a similar section in the volume on *Hebrews* in the *New International Commentary on the New Testament* by F.F. Bruce.]

1:1-14

God spoke in various ways at various times and various places to our fathers through the prophets in times past, but now He has spoken His final word to us through a Son, His perfect representative. This Son is heir, participated in the creation, bears the splendor and nature of the Father, and is now active in sustaining all things, having purified sin and having been exalted by God. The Son of God is greater than any of the prophets; he is also greater than the angels, as the ancient Scriptures clearly testify.

2:1-18

Pay attention! It was through angels that Moses' law was communicated, and its sanctions were very severe; how much more perilous is it to ignore the saving message brought not by angels, but by Jesus, the Son of God, the Lord. This message was confirmed by witnesses and by God the Father in various ways.

Jesus, the Son of God, is the One to whom the dominion of the world has been committed for all time to come. This is how it happened. Psalm 8 tells us that God put everything under the dominion of human beings, but now not everything is subject to human beings. With the entry of sin, human beings lost control of death. Therefore, this Son of God, becoming also Son of Man, had to take upon Himself human nature and suffer death for all humanity in order to win back the dominion that was lost through sin. To do this He had to conquer the devil who had falsely usurped death, and he had to rescue those who were held in bondage to this false power. He conquered the devil when He invaded the realm of death through his own death. The devil had controlled death until then, but Jesus conquered death and thereby overpowered Satan. Because Jesus took the form of human beings, he is qualified to serve as a merciful high priest on behalf of all mankind; he knows all about human trials from his own experiences and can give timely help to meet human needs. Because Jesus is Son of God, he is also a faithful high priest whose sacrifice makes possible the forgiveness of the sins of the people.

3:1-4:13

Jesus, sent by God to be a high priest, deserves more attention and honor in the house of God than Moses. Jesus is faithful as a son in God's house, Moses was faithful as a servant. In fact, Moses testified about Jesus when he testified of things that were to come.

Watch out! Be faithful! Those who rebelled against God during the wilderness wanderings were excluded from rest in the Promised Land because of their hard hearts, unbelief and disobedience. Because David in the Psalms wrote about the rest still available in his day, we know there remains a better rest than that which the Israelites were promised in Canaan. That better rest still awaits God's people.

We must take care not to forfeit this rest by rebelling against God when He speaks to us. The message must be combined with faith and obedience. God's rest is still available. Let us make every effort to enter that rest. Now God speaks, not through his servant Moses as he did in those days, but through His Son, who is greater than Moses. That message is powerful because God knows and sees everything.

4:14-6:12

As already explained, Jesus as Son of God is a great high priest who deals with sin. He is also able to sympathize with and help his people. He has been called to his high-priestly office by God Himself, in the order of Melchizedek, as is made clear in inspired Scripture. Jesus perfectly represents God as Son of God, and he perfectly represents humanity in his participation in the human experience, especially in his struggle with death.

I urge you, Grow Up! I would like to say more, but I do not think I can because of your spiritual immaturity. I urge you to think maturely and move beyond the basics. I warn you that some who had tasted the blessings of the new age reached a point where they could never be brought back, because even after falling they continued to reject and disgrace God's Son. Not that I think you are considering such; I have a better hope for you than that. Press on; reach for maturity and do not get stuck or slip back.

6:13-20

Christ is divinely appointed a high priest of Melchizedek's order, and that by the oath of God. You remember the story. God made a promise to Abraham and confirmed it with an oath. It was doubly certain—because God said it and he cannot lie, and because God sealed it with an oath. We have this same hope, based on God's promise; it is still valid. Jesus' entry into the presence of God as our forerunner is evidence that we too can draw near.

7:1-28

Let me return to the Melchizedek story even though you already know it. Melchizedek appears without antecedent, and nothing more is said about him afterward. He was a very great man; our father Abraham paid him tithes and received his blessing. You might even say that Levi, ancestor of the priestly families of Israel, paid Melchizedek tithes in the person of Abraham. This implies that Melchizedek is greater than Levi, and Melchizedek's priesthood greater than Aaron's. If perfect, complete access to God had been attained under the Aaronic priesthood, why would God have designated the Messiah as priest according to a different order later?

Jesus' priesthood is superior to Aaron's in many ways. First, Jesus was confirmed to the office by the oath of God. Second, Jesus is immortal whereas Aaronic priests died. Jesus is sinless; the priests of Aaron's line had to present a personal sin-offering to cleanse themselves before presenting the offering for the people. Jesus' sacrifice was "once for all" and did not have to be repeated whereas the Aaronic priestly service required repeated sacrifices. The result of Jesus' sacrifice was a better hope by which we draw near to God. The replacement of the priesthood made necessary a replacement of the law.

8:1-10:18

The point of what I am saying is this: we have a high priest just like this. Jesus is the high priest and mediator of a new and better covenant, for he is continually before God, seated at his right hand, serving in the true sanctuary of the true dwelling of God. The introduction of a new covenant means the former one is obsolete because of its defects. The former system was a copy and shadow of heavenly realities. The old covenant provided for the removal of external pollution through animal sacrifices and various rites, but could never remove sin. The way to full access to the Most Holy Place was not clear under the old order. The blood of Jesus, an acceptable "once for all" sacrifice, cleanses the conscience from guilt and thus abolishes the barrier between people and God. This was never possible under the previous priesthood and covenant. In the heavenly sanctuary, there is no barrier like the curtain in the old covenant; direct access to God is available through Jesus in a spiritual, eternal order of which the earthly sanctuary was only a temporary and inadequate copy.

10:19-12:3

Since we can now enter the Most Holy Place, approaching the very presence of God, by a new and living way through the blood of Jesus, we should abandon the old obsolescent order.

It is as though God is saying to us, Come Here! Draw near! We respond because of God's promises and because God is faithful. This is no time to shrink back and stay away from God. Let us maintain hope and faith, firmly assured of eternal realities that are invisible. We look forward with eager expectation, with the same forward-looking faith of earlier saints who gained God's approval. They lived awaiting the fulfillment of promises that have become reality in our day. They give testimony of God's faithfulness. Let us follow their example; better yet, let us throw off the weight and the sin, running the race with endurance, following the example of Jesus, pursuing God faithfully.

12:4-13:25

Let us not grow faint-hearted in our trials; these are proof that we are sons of God.

Don't miss it! It is possible to miss out on the grace of God. Our heritage in this age of fulfillment is glorious, far surpassing what happened in days gone by under the first covenant.

How can we consider going back? We are receiving an immovable kingdom! Maintain your confession in faith and patience, imitating those who went before, and depending on God who raised Jesus from the dead.

Studies, Sermon Starters, and Notes

Note: Some of the material in this section has been collected over several years from a variety of sources. No claim is made to originality. Help in identifying original sources will be appreciated and appropriate credit given in future editions.

The items included here have two purposes. First, they provide a summary of the of the primary themes of the book, thus suggesting content for classes and sermons. Second, they suggest some ways in which the text can be presented in the move from the text to the sermon or class.

Sermon
Portraits of Jesus
Descriptions which emphasize his Divinity
- Son of God, 1:2-3, 3:6, 4:14, 5:5-10, et.al.
- Heir of all things, 1:2
- Creator of the universe, 1:2
- Ruler, seated at right hand of majesty in heaven, 1:3
- Sustainer of all things, 1:3 [glue, holding things together]
- Radiance of God's glory, 1:3
- Exact representation of God's being, 1:3

Descriptions which focus on his role as Savior
- Purification for sins, 1:3
- Author of salvation, 2:10
- High priest, 2:17, 3:1, 4:14, 5:1-10, et.al. [Makes atonement, 2:17]
- Apostle, 3:1 [sent from God]
- Source of eternal salvation, 5:9
- Guarantee of better covenant, 7:22
- Savior, 7:25
- Sacrifice, 9:14
- Mediator of new covenant, 9:15

Descriptions which emphasize his Humanity
- Made a little lower than the angels, 2:9
- Brother, 2:11, 17
- Nourisher, 2:18, 4:14-16 [human side]
- Author and finisher [perfecter] of our faith, 12:2

Study
What is Hebrews About?
We want a book that is relevant. What is this book about?
- Jesus Christ, 1-2
- Belief, unbelief, and keeping on, 3-4
- Growing and Progressing, 5-6
- Clean conscience and close relationships, 7-10:18
- Encouraging and urging, 10:19-39
- Faith and perseverance, 11-12 (what is permanent, immovable, eternal)
- How we live our lives, 13

It is about....
- Understanding and sharing faith in Jesus
- Developing biblical faith
- Encouraging and persevering

The goal is spiritual rejuvenation

Sermon
Hebrews: A Word of Exhortation
The purpose of Hebrews is to exhort, console, literally to be "by the side of"

Jesus, Son of God, 1:1-2:4
       Exhortation: Listen, 2:1-4
Jesus, Son of Man, 2:5-18

Jesus, faithful high priest, 3:1-4:13
       Exhortation: develop faith and faithfulness, 3:11-12

Jesus, merciful high priest, 4:14-5:10
       Exhortation: grow up to maturity, 5:11-6:12
       Excursus: God's word and God's oath, foundations for faith and hope, 6:13-20
Jesus, "Melchizedek" high priest, 7:1-28

Jesus the high priest: better ministry, better covenant, better promises, 8:1-6
Jesus brings a better covenant with better sacrifice, 8:7-10:18

Jesus brings better promises, 10:19-12:29
>Call to draw near without shrinking, 10:19-39
>Exhortation: draw near, hold fast, encourage, 10:22-25
>Call to faith in the promises, 11
>Call to perseverance, 12
>Exhortation: be careful, 12:14-16

Call to Christian living with numerous imperatives, 13

Sermon
The Exhortations of the book of Hebrews
In Christ, God completes his revelation, 1:1-4
This demonstrates that Jesus in his character exists in a category that is superior to—

- The angels, 1:4-2:18
- Moses, 3:1-4:13
- The Levitical priesthood, 4:14-7:25

Lessons from the exhortations
[2:1-4; 3:12-13; 5:11-14; 10:22-25; 12:14-16; multiple imperatives in chapter 13]

- 2:1-4, be diligent, it is easy to slip, it is easy to pay too little attention to salvation
- 3:12-13, guard your heart against evil and unbelief; it is dangerous to separate yourself, guard against the deceit of sin, unbelief leads to disobedience
- 5:11-14, have an open heart, seek maturity, be careful and guard against a lack of spirituality
- 10:22-25, draw near, be firm, consider others, stimulate to love and good works, exhort
- 12:14-16, take off the weights and burdens, "run," put your eyes on Jesus, make the sacrifice, be very careful

Conclusion, 12:22-29

- Living God
- God as just judge
- Jesus as mediator of New Testament
- Sprinkled blood leads to a clean conscience
- The immovable things stand and will stand
- Thanksgiving
- Serve God with fear and reverence

Study
Why is a study of Hebrews important?
Hebrews is relevant and needed, especially for those who are described by these phrases:
- Attracted by world
- Losing faith
- Experiencing tragedy and loss
- Losing first love
- Have made lots of sacrifices in the past
- Religion has become ritual, just doing the motions
- Lack of growth
- Christianity without heart
- Without the desire to grow
- Without the power to minister
- Needing to be awakened again
- In need of vitality, tired
- Lost the dream

What is the Answer? Hebrews is about—
- Jesus
- Faith
- Growth
- Perseverance
- Encouragement

Hebrews is about—
- God's forgiveness (pardon)
- God's new plan (pact)
- God's promises

Sermon
Heeding the Warnings from Hebrews
Hebrews concentrates on Jesus. One must understand the significance and centrality of Jesus Christ. Failing to properly understand Jesus is a danger to faith. There are various danger points. It is easy to dwell in the shadows and miss the substance, to erect a shadowy reality with no substance. One book on Hebrews is titled, *From Shadow to Substance.* How does one tell the difference between a substitute and the real thing?

The book of Hebrews is often outlined around five major warnings:

2:1   Therefore we must pay closer attention--JESUS
3:12 Do not turn away from the living God--FAITH
5:11 Grow up--GOD'S WORD
10:19 Draw near to God in full assurance--WORSHIP
12:14 Don't miss God's grace--RELATIONSHIP WITH GOD
      Here are five important principles with lessons for life. Shadow is nothing--substance is everything.

Sermon
Jesus—Faithful and Merciful High Priest, 2:17-18
<u>There are two aspects of the high priesthood of Jesus (Heb. 2:17-18)</u>
      First, because he is Son of God, he is a faithful high priest and can make expiation for the sins of the people.
      Second, because he is Son of Man, he is a merciful high priest and can understand and succor human beings who are tempted and face problems.
<u>Jesus can help with two difficulties that are a common part of life (Heb. 12:1-2)</u>
      Because he is a merciful high priest, he can help with the pressures and difficulties of life, the things that entangle us and make us stumble. Because he is a faithful high priest, he can help with the sin that so easily besets us.

Sermon
When God's Church Doesn't Grow, 5:11-14
- Spiritually
- In knowledge
- In power
- In ministry
- In focus
- In faith

Sermon
How to Remain Firm in Faith, 5:11-6:12
- The problem "you" have
- The commitments "we" have
- The experience "they" had
- The better things "you" will have

Study

The Problem of Losing Faith—The Problem of Reviving a Tired Church

[The numerical references in parentheses are to the primary exhortations in the book]

Introduction: Losing faith in God, in Jesus Christ, in others, in the church, in the future—lack of hope. How and why do we lose faith?

1-2. Cannot see Jesus; do not know word of God; failure to see finality of revelation (#1)
- Cannot see the reality of the victory
- Do not depend on source of help
  - Must recognize the great salvation
  - Must look to the merciful and faithful high priest

3-4. Weariness of journey
- Disbelief, lack of consequences in daily life (#2)
- Lack of a long-term view
  - Must hear God's Word

5-7. Failure to appreciate salvation
- Lack of maturity (#3)
- Lack of hope in the promises
  - Must seek to grow, mature
  - Must wait on the promises

8-10:18. Cannot see the greater-superior-better
- Christ sees and cares and intercedes
- Christ is coming

10:19-12:29. Lack of drawing near (#4)
- Lack of fellowship or assembly; lack of assuring faith and long-term vision
- Lack of focus on Jesus; not understanding the nature of the world and discipline
- Not acting on the promises (#5); cannot see the reason for faith in God
  - Hold on to the prize
  - Keep faith
  - Endure and persevere

Renew our commitments

Sermon

Strength for the Journey: Imitating Christ, Hebrews 12

Most of us have a problem with perseverance. How do we keep on keeping on?

-1- Practice the presence of Jesus (fix our eyes on Jesus) Look to Jesus. FOCUS.

- WHO: Jesus and the "cloud of witnesses"
- Learn from the examples of those who went before us, throw aside the hindrances,
- Run the race with patience, look to Jesus constantly, and follow his example.

-2- Practice spiritual discipline; the "soul life" (vv. 4-11). Learn discipline. TRAINING.

- WHO: You and God
- Do not make light of the task, do not lose heart, persevere, and learn holiness.

-3- Practice self-examination. Examine self, be honest (vv. 11-13). SELF-EVALUATION.

- WHO: You by yourself
- Strengthen the feeble and weak places, don't make life harder than it is
- Don't put stumbling blocks in your way or the way of others.

-4- Practice spiritual exercise. Commit to being stretched (vv. 14-17). EXERCISE.

- WHO: You and others
- Live in peace with all; be holy; don't miss grace of God; avoid bitterness
- No sexual immorality or godlessness

-5- Worship God (comparison of Sinai and Zion). WORSHIP.

- WHO: You and God
- Do not refuse God, reject things that can be "shaken," cling to the "unshakable."
- See God, honor Jesus, and gratefully worship.

Heb. 12: here is power for transformation, in the faith of God Do not quit. That is the message of Hebrews; we take this message to the world most effectively when we live it out in our daily lives.

Sermon
Encouragement, Hebrews 10:19-25
The theme of encouragement occurs frequently in the book of Hebrews (3:13;
6:18; 10:25; 12:5; 13:22). How can the Christian find encouragement?
See the Possibilities
- Draw near, walk close to God with confidence
See the Positives
- Hold fast
See the Potential
- Build one another up
Conclusion: Focus on spiritual realities, persevere in spiritual faith-
fulness, and encourage spiritual growth—all by faith

Sermon
**Lessons to be Learned by Looking at the Faith of Others, He-
brews 11**
Four competing systems for guiding life
- Emotions
- Situations
- Tradition
- Revelation
Lessons from the faith experiences described in Hebrews 11
- Do not blame problems on the past
- The present is not the final word, the final result
- The future depends on God

Sermon
**Did anything happen when you decided to follow Christ? 12:18-
29**
There is a huge difference between the experience of Israel in the
Old Testament and the experience of God's people under the New
Testament
- 22, the presence of God, personal relationship with the living God is possible
- 23, a different view of God, the just judge that makes the
  righteous complete
- 24, Jesus, a mediator that makes it possible for us to approach God
- 24, clean consciences are possible
- 28, an immovable kingdom
- 29, genuine hope

Sermon
The Nature of Faith, Hebrews 11

Two aspects of faith are described in 11:1—certainty of hope and confidence in things not seen. These two ideas are constantly intertwined in Hebrews 11.

- Illustrations related to things not seen, vv. 2-5
- The two aspects of faith are mentioned again in v. 6
- Illustrations that combine promise/hope and things not seen, vv. 7-8
- Illustrations that focus on hope in God's promise of the future, vv. 9-22
- Illustrations focused on Moses, vv. 23-29
- Multiplied illustrations, vv. 24-38

Faith does not have to receive the promise, faith only has to believe the promise, to know that what is now invisible will one day be visible. Faith testifies that God is in control, vv. 39-40.

Sermon
Abraham, Hebrews 11

11:8 "Abraham. . .obeyed" In some ways these cameos are idealized representations of these men's lives. The OT is unique in ancient literature in that it records both the positive and negative about its characters. Abraham was a strange mixture of fear and faith

Fear
- God said leave your family; he took his father and Lot
- God promised a child; he tried to produce a child through Sarah's servant and later tried to give Sarah away to both an Egyptian and a Philistine king in order to save his own life

Faith
- He did leave Ur
- He did believe God would give him descendants
- He was willing to offer Isaac (cf. Gen. 22)

God is not looking for "super-saints," but for flawed humans who will respond to Him in repentance and faith and live for Him regardless of the circumstances.

Sermon
A Plan for Life: Life in the Power of God's Promise, Hebrews 13:8-21

In Hebrews, doctrinal foundations lead to peaks of practical exhortation. We come to the end of the book; we expect exhortation and practical living. Doctrine comes full-circle. There is doctrine—but the focus is on how you live life. Look at the imperatives in this chapter.

The author in this concluding chapter says 6 things about life. Life is...

- Daily, the daily life, 1-6
- Disciplined, the disciplined life, 7-14
- Worshipful, the worshipful life, 15
- Holy, the focused life, 18
- Empowered, the equipped life, 20-21
- Shared, the shared life, 7, 17, 23-24

Life Is Daily Discipline (1-8)

No hit and miss, no here today and gone tomorrow, no maybes.

- Keep on loving...
- Don't forget...
- Remember those in prison and mistreated...
- Honor marriage...
- Avoid covetousness, love of money...be content
- Remember your leaders...
- Consider their example...
- Imitate them...

How do you do it? Live in the priorities of God. Live in the presence of Christ. Today....

Life Is Holy Worship (9-19)

Do not forget to do good and share with others; Live a sacrificial life.

- Obey leaders...submit to authority
- Obey
- Pray...

Life Is Shared Empowerment (20-25)

- We look to the future, forever.

www.ingramcontent.com/pod-product-compliance
Lightning Source LLC
Chambersburg PA
CBHW071602040426
42452CB00008B/1258